# AROUND THE WORLD IN 40 FEET

TWO HUNDRED DAYS IN
THE LIFE OF A 40FT NYK
SHIPPING CONTAINER

BY **RICHARD COOK**
AND **MARCUS OLENIUK**

# Foreword

*It gives me great pleasure to be penning this foreword. Around the World in 40 Feet follows 200 days in the life of one NYK blue box as it crisscrosses the globe, moving our customers' goods from one end of the planet to the other. It is an intriguing and unique way to look at our industry that takes us on an amazing journey spanning six continents and covering almost 125,000 kilometers and in so doing, I feel it goes to the very heart of our business.*

*Around the World in 40 Feet shows how, by forging strong connections between different peoples, cultures, and technologies, NYK is working hard to bring real value to the world.*

*This book was a bold undertaking for NYK. It took more than a year to complete and involved hard work from a lot of our people across the globe. Here, I would like to take the opportunity to thank all the NYK personnel involved. The effort was considerable but the results, I think, speak for themselves. A sincere thanks to you all.*

*I would also like to thank the editorial team of writer Richard Cook and photographer Marcus Oleniuk, and their publishing team at WordAsia in Hong Kong. Richard and Marcus traveled the world for this project, and it is because of their dedicated efforts that this book became a reality. From all of us at NYK, thank you.*

*Finally, I would like to thank our many customers who kindly helped us with their patient and generous assistance. The movement of a shipping container is, for most of us, a crucial yet unexciting part of our business. Around the World in 40 Feet provides us all with a wonderful opportunity to see things differently. I also sincerely hope it shows how NYK has developed into the finest integrated logistics provider in the world.*

*I hope you enjoy the book.*

Hiroyuki Shimizu
Senior Managing Director
NYK Line

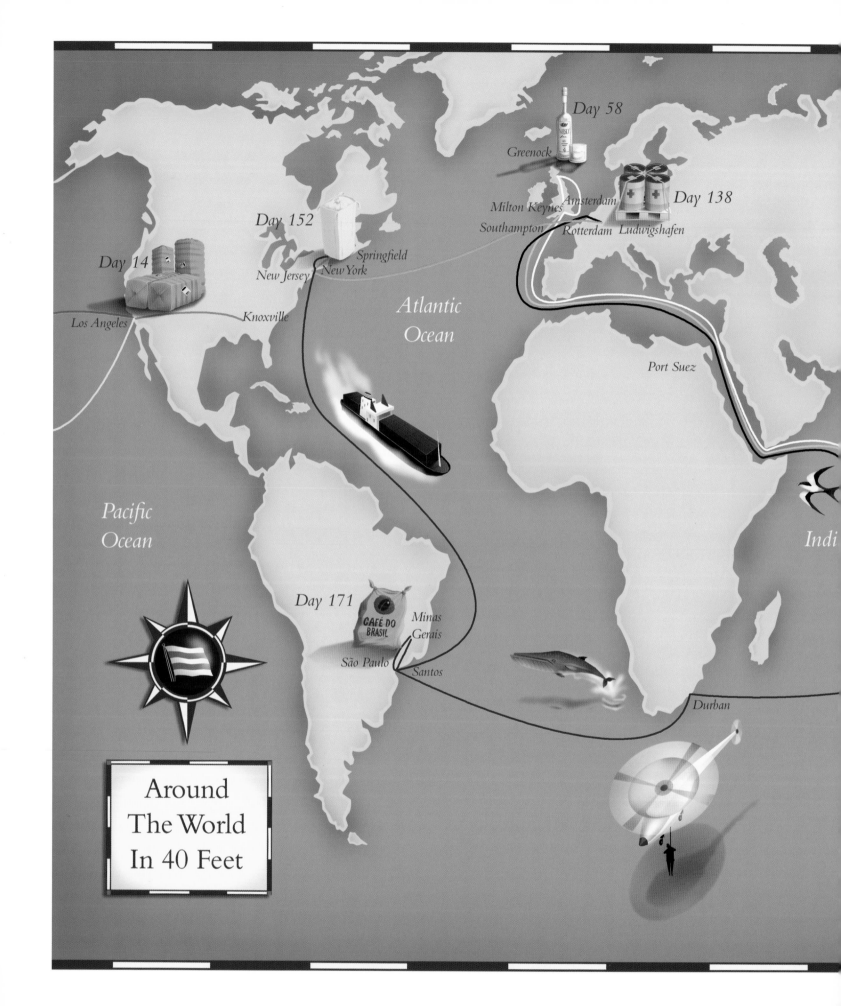

Day 58

Greenock

Day 152

Day 14

Los Angeles

Springfield
New Jersey New York

Knoxville

Milton Keynes Amsterdam
Southampton Rotterdam Ludwigshafen

Day 138

Atlantic
Ocean

Port Suez

Pacific
Ocean

Indi

Day 171

CAFÉ DO
BRASIL

Minas
Gerais

São Paulo Santos

Durban

Around
The World
In 40 Feet

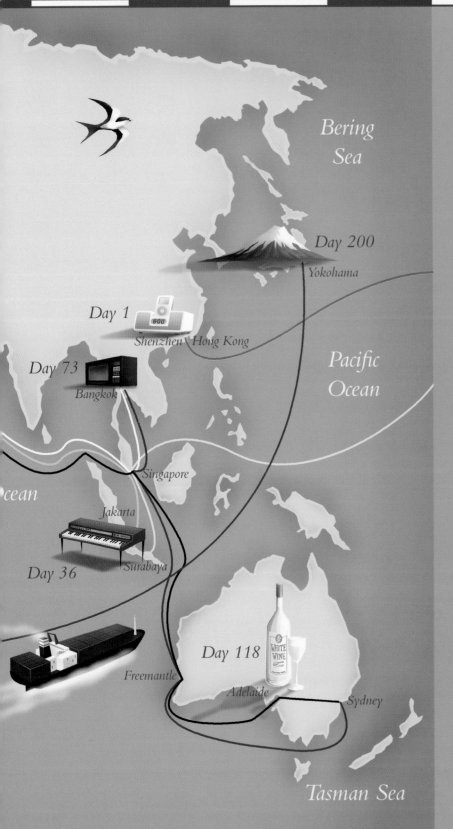

Bering
Sea

Day 200

Yokohama

Day 1

Shenzhen Hong Kong

Pacific
Ocean

Day 73

Bangkok

Singapore

cean

Jakarta

Day 36

Surabaya

Day 118

Freemantle

Adelaide

Sydney

Tasman Sea

# THE VOYAGE

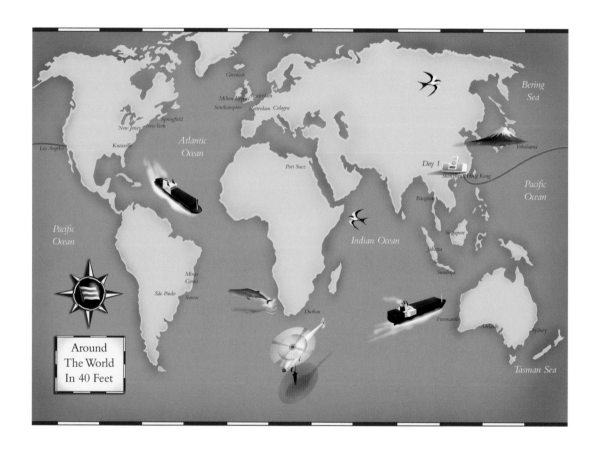

*Radio Alarm Clocks*
*Shenzhen–Hong Kong–Los Angeles*

# Chapter 1

## DAY **1**, KILOMETER **1**
# SHENZHEN, CHINA

I t's early evening, it's warm and humid and the streets of Shenzhen are busy with life. The pavements, street-side stores and tiny, hole-in-the-wall eateries are filled with groups of noisy, joking young factory workers who, having just finished their shifts, are trying to make the most of their night-time freedom. The roads are crowded too, as scores of bicycles and motorbikes jostle for space with cars, jeeps and trucks in the labyrinth of gray lanes and highways that dissect this unremitting industrial maze of squat, low-rise blocks.

At a Yantian container yard, within sight of the tall cranes busy working in the port across the road, a line of trucks queue as they wait to leave. Each truck carries an empty container; by tomorrow lunchtime, all the containers in the queue will have been filled. By the following day, all will be on ships. The first box in the queue will be heading west to Suez and then Hamburg, the second southeast to Panama and then New Jersey and the third, box number NYKU 596079–1, will be going east across the North Pacific to Los Angeles.

Box NYKU 596079–1 pulls up to the gate and its interior is checked. It's good: it is clean, the floor and sides are undamaged and there is no lingering smell inside. Then the top is checked, via an overhead gantry, as is the underbelly, and both are sound. The box's number is then matched to the information that the gatehouse staff pull up on a roadside computer screen. The truck is cleared to leave the yard and is driven a few blocks around the corner to an NYK Logistics distribution center, where it waits overnight with more than 30 other NYK containers. Just after 08.00 the next morning it is backed up to a loading bay; within five minutes a team of four are energetically packing the box tightly with scores of plain cardboard cartons.

The goods being loaded into the line of NYK containers on this cloudy, dark South China morning are for one customer, one of the largest American retail store chains, and are mainly

household items – lamps, fans, gift-wrapping paper, barbecue tongs, dinner place mats – that will, over the coming months, end up in homes across the United States.

Box NYKU 596079–1 is loaded with three different types of goods: coffee makers, humidifiers and small, personal stereo-compatible radio alarm clocks. The U.S. retailer has had them made at different specialist assembly plants across Shenzhen while these assembly plants have, in turn, purchased the mountains of components from dozens of other nearby factories.

It's a relentless yet efficient manufacturing and distribution system. The components first arrive at the factory in rack after rack of small plastic trays before leaving a few days later as part of the finished item, packed inside plain cardboard cartons marked only with a cipher of barcodes, product numbers and the abbreviated name of their American destination.

From the factory, the goods are taken to the distribution center, the NYK Yantian logistics warehouse, where they are grouped into container-sized orders that are then dispatched directly – by road, ship and rail – to the customer's numerous distribution centers across the States.

The packing is done within an hour and then the box heads south, for 100 kilometers, to the Port of Hong Kong, ready to be loaded aboard the L.A.-bound NYK Kai in the morning.

Modern container ports, like the cargo holds on modern container ships, are essentially physical manifestations of complex computer programs that appear on screens as coded grids of colors, numbers and rows; all contain a wealth of constantly updated information used by customs, customer, port and shipper alike.

However, look at a modern-day port for real, and from afar it's like some kind of straight-edged metallic ants nest. Thousands of containers sit stacked in neat rows as armies of trucks and mobile cranes gracefully glide between them in radio- and computer-controled synchronicity, moving the boxes from the stacks to the gates or to the larger, towering cranes that line the wharves. Those cranes effortlessly pluck the containers, then deposit them in the holds of the waiting ships.

More than 16 million containers move through the nine terminals at Hong Kong's Kwai Chung Container Terminals every year. It's a system that has to work well – and it does. NYKU 596079–1 is in the port holding stacks before 21.00. By 08.40 the next day it is swinging in the air, about to be lowered into cargo bay Number 3 on the NYK Kai. By 15.30 it has left Asia. Next stop, Los Angeles.

**ABOVE** – Like so many of today's container voyages, this 125,000-kilometer story starts in southern China, where box NYKU 596079–1 is quickly filled at NYK's busy Yantian logistics warehouse. Goods arrive here on an hourly basis from a network of different specialist assembly plants and are consolidated into container-size orders that are then rapidly dispatched to all corners of the planet.

**OPPOSITE PAGE** – The box is cleared by customs and sealed before it leaves Yantian, by road, for Hong Kong port. The next time it is opened it will be in California… and its load of coffee-makers, humidifiers and alarm clocks will be in American stores and homes within weeks of leaving China.

The packing is done within an hour and then the box heads south, for 100 kilometers, to the Port of Hong Kong. By 08.40 the next day it is swinging in the air, about to be lowered into cargo bay Number 3 on the NYK Kai; by 15.30 it has left Asia. Next stop, Los Angeles.

**ABOVE –** Hong Kong port's nine bustling terminals, all sited near the heart of the city, move more than 16 million containers a year.

**OPPOSITE PAGE –** Fast turnarounds and tight terminal schedules mean port visits are now the busiest part of a mariner's working life.

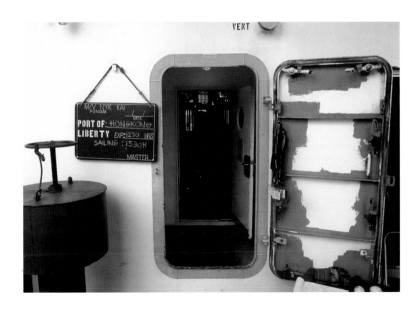

## DAY **12**, KILOMETER **10,325**
# LOS ANGELES, USA

I t's lunchtime in south Los Angeles and, as box NYKU
596079–1 arrives at the NYK Logistics Center in
Carson, some of the warehouse workers are about to
enjoy an alfresco lunch under the bright blue, classically
clear Californian sky.

The lingua franca at Carson, like most other places across
South L.A., is a wonderfully expressive English and Spanish
hybrid. A mobile diner, which pulls into the compound every
day and serves delicious, freshly made Mexican fare, is the ever-
popular venue of choice among the Carson staff.

Over at the yard's entrance, a gatehouse supervisor – who
has yet to take his lunch break – walks along an overhead
gantry that straddles the gate and places a magnetic sensor
onto the corner of NYKU 596079–1's roof before waving it
into the complex.

Box NYKU 596079–1 landed in the United States just
15 kilometers down the road at Yusen Terminals (YTI) in the
Port of Los Angeles and was pulled from the NYK Kai at 18.30
after the ship's 10-day passage from Hong Kong. It left YTI this
morning but before it started moving to Carson along L.A.'s
notoriously busy Route 710, the YTI port operations system
sent an electronic note to a team of vessel coordinators based
at Carson, which carried the container's "where, what and
when" information. Once its movement from port to Carson
was confirmed, the vessel coordinators passed this information
on to the team of warehouse controllers, who in turn sent the
information to the sensor-placing gate crews.

"The sensors mean we always know where a box is,"
explains David Garcia, Operations Manager at the yard. "Once
it is through these gates, our warehouse controllers can pull its
number up on a screen and know where it is, what needs to
happen to it next and, with the press of a button, can remotely
call in a driver to move it to a loading bay.

"As you can see, this is a busy place," continues David as he points to the sea of containers surrounding him. "We can have as many as 1,200 full containers in here and tracking is vital to our operation."

Carson is what is known as a "cross-dock" facility. Goods come here from the port in 20-foot and 40-foot international containers and leave again in standard American domestic 53-foot trailers, normally heading to one of the many rail yards dotted across the south L.A. area, where they will be put aboard a freight train to be taken somewhere in the States.

The complex is effectively a giant parking lot that surrounds a much smaller set of warehouse buildings, and the goods remain stored in their containers until the customer informs Carson that they are needed. Then the international container is taken to a loading bay next to its respective domestic trailer – either side by side, or before sets of facing doors – and the goods are "cross-docked" from one box to another.

"If we are doing our jobs correctly, at the end of each day the warehouse floor should be as good as empty," says David. "Everything should be either loaded and gone or still in its container waiting to be unloaded."

NYKU 596079–1 is one of the first in a batch of 32 containers that will arrive at Carson today from the NYK yard in Yantian, via the NYK Kai. Some will then wait for days in the yard; others will be pulled up to the banks of loading bays within hours of arriving at the complex. NYKU 596079–1 waits just one day.

Once it is pulled up to the loading bays its contents are transferred, within 40 minutes, to a domestic trailer that leaves the complex almost immediately and heads to a Union Pacific Rail Yard 20 minutes' drive away, where it connects with a 220-container-long freight train.

The train will carry it first to Arkansas, where it will be transferred to a train bound for Tennessee. Within three weeks of leaving Shenzhen, and after traveling almost 12,000 kilometers, the alarm radios, coffee makers and humidifiers will be in the customer's distribution center in the city of Knoxville.

Now empty, Box NYKU 596079–1 spends a few more hours in the Carson yard before having its sensor removed at the gate and departing. It heads a few kilometers across the sun-soaked concrete sprawl that is suburban South L.A. to a warehouse in Compton, where it is filled with 85 bales of premium-quality Californian cotton.

Next, NYKU 596079–1 is going to Indonesia.

**ABOVE –** After arriving in the United States, Box NYKU 596079–1 is opened in South Los Angeles, at NYK's "cross-dock" facility in Long Beach, where goods are moved directly from container to trailer: out of the 20- and 40-foot international containers that arrive from the port, and straight into the 53-foot domestic trailers that then leave, normally by rail, for points across the States.

**OPPOSITE PAGE –** David Garcia (center), Operations Manager at NYK's Carson Logistics Center, oversees a huge yard that at any one time can hold more than 1,200 containers. The facility makes use of a centrally run real-time location system that controls all container movements within the complex.

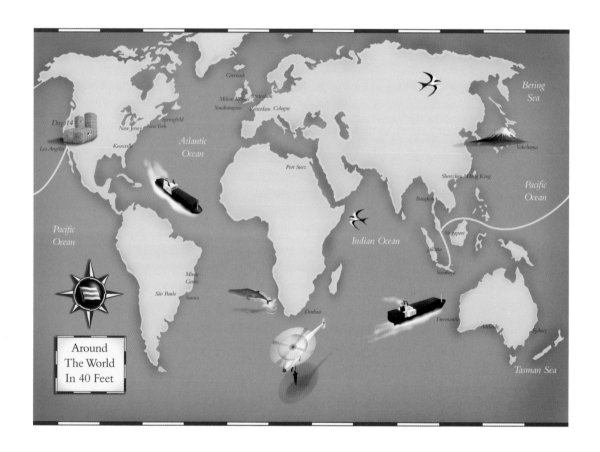

*Raw Cotton*
*Los Angeles–Singapore–Surabaya*

# Chapter 2

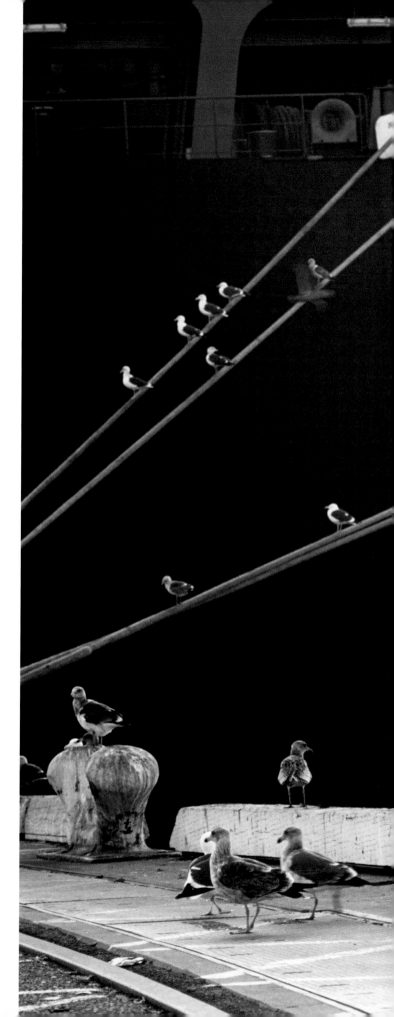

## DAY **14**, KILOMETER **10,350**
# LOS ANGELES, USA

Crane operator Marty Lopez leans forward and looks directly below him at the Yusen Terminals quay, 30 meters down. Then, with arms reaching out to the controls on either side of him and feet deftly working the pedals on the thick glass floor, he neatly lifts NYKU 596079–1 up and away from American soil and safely onto the NYK Libra. Marty, who comes from four generations of longshoremen, chuckles when told that the box is filled with cotton.

"I started working as a longshoreman in 1975 when I left high school. We loaded a lot of cotton in those days and it was before containerization had really taken off," he says. "Then, a load of cotton bales would be dropped into the middle of a ship's hull and teams would manually pull them into position using hooks. It took all day and needed up to 100 men."

At Yusen Terminals, things are now very different. The team moving today's cotton includes Marty in the crane; a small team on the ground guiding the truck, checking the container number and placing the twist locks – which fix the containers in position when stacked – into the bottom four corners of each box; plus another small team on the ship checking that each box is correctly stowed. With fewer than 10 men, the cotton moves from quay to ship's hold in less than two minutes.

However, despite all the changes, today's work is far from easy. Marty has to work hard to keep up with the incessant arrival of trucks appearing way below him while also keeping a vigilant eye on the activities and movements of his teammates on the ship's decks.

"Safety overrides everything," he says emphatically. He has to speak up to be heard over the whine of the crane's cables, the deep clank of heavy metal in transit and the alarm bells that constantly ring, indicating a container or a crane is, once again, on the move.

"The trick to it," he explains, "is to try to keep the movement constant. If the whole team keeps moving, the speed will always be good enough."

Marty then points along the line of the ship below him, showing how the stern is a little higher than the bow, which means the deck is not flat.

"That makes things a bit more difficult… it's because the cargo weight is currently a little uneven," he explains as he heaves another container into the air.

Up on the bridge of the NYK Libra is the ship's second officer, Wilson Alzaga. Like Marty, Wilson has also become aware of the slightly uneven loading pattern. He looks at a console and, with the experienced flick of a few buttons, takes in water ballast to rectify things. "No big deal," says Wilson calmly.

Right now, more of a concern to Wilson is the weather in the North Pacific Ocean. The Libra was late arriving from Tokyo because of rough weather and is heading back to Tokyo and on to Yokohama, Hong Kong and then Singapore.

The shortest route between the two continents heads far north across the Pacific, cutting below the Aleutian Islands and the Gulf of Alaska. However, when the weather is bad – which unsurprisingly is regular in the North Pacific – ships often favor the more southerly route that, at more than 8,200 kilometers, adds about 300 kilometers to the trip and, of course, extra fuel costs.

For the run back to Asia, the Libra's captain Torsten Olbrich has chosen the southerly route and Wilson points out the projected path on one of the ship's charts.

"This way, we stay out of the way of the weather," he says, tracing a line that goes marginally closer to Hawaii than it does to Alaska. "We cover more distance but we should make up time."

By the time Marty Lopez has started work next day the Libra is loaded and ready to depart. And Captain Olbrich's hunch was right. After leaving Los Angeles the ship sails across the North Pacific in less than 10 days and continues to make good time through the East China Sea and the Luzon Strait, and south through the South China Sea, before arriving in Singapore, just two hours behind schedule.

Box NYKU 596079–1 then spends 16 hours in the Port of Singapore before being loaded aboard the ACX Sumire and heading south, through the Natuna Sea. It arrives at the Port of Surabaya, Indonesia, just as dusk is falling and the mosque's call to evening prayer floats across the rapidly darkening dock.

**ABOVE –** Box NYKU 596079–1, on its way to pick up cotton in Compton, heads past one of the many railheads that ring Los Angeles. While trucks move containers between port terminals and warehouses, it is trains that carry out more than 90% of NYK's long-distance U.S. container moves.

**OPPOSITE PAGE –** At a cotton transload facility in Compton, Los Angeles, NYK Account Manager John Greene (top), who has been handling the global movement of Californian cotton for two decades, watches as another consignment is successfully loaded for export.

## DAY **26**, KILOMETER **24,870**
# MOJOKERTO, INDONESIA

I t's just after daybreak. Sitting on the roof of NYKU 596079–1 is a small flock of swallows; they are making the most of the balmy morning breeze by continually diving, one after another, off the container, then soaring gracefully between a set of tall storage sheds and a pair of gently swaying palm trees before returning to the container roof, ready to go round again.

The box has been in Indonesia for less than 36 hours. After being unloaded from the ACX Sumire it spent its first night at the port in Surabaya. On clearing customs it traveled south by road for two bumpy hours, to a cotton mill in the leafy district of Mojokerto, where it spent last night in a secure parking lot at the front of the factory compound. At dawn, the box was driven round to the tall storage shed where it now sits.

The sheds are piled high with hundreds of sacks of raw Californian cotton; inside, there is the same, unmistakable smell that lingered at the warehouse in Compton 13,000 kilometers ago – the distinctively earthy and not necessarily unpleasant scent of raw cotton mixed with jute sacking.

Once a four-man unloading team has appeared – but not before the factory's import supervisor is on the scene and has given the all-important nod – the container's seal is cut, the doors are swung open and a forklift truck is nudged against the first few bales so they gently tumble from the container.

Then, one of the team climbs up into the box and clambers over a pile of bales, hauling a steel hawser behind him. He loops it around as many of the bales as he can and, when they are secure – and he is out of the way – he blows the whistle clamped between his teeth.

The other end of the hawser is swiftly attached to the forklift truck; there is another blast from another whistle, and

the truck quickly reverses. As it does so, more than a dozen bales of American cotton come bouncing from the container out into the bright Indonesian morning.

The team repeats the hawser-and-pull procedure until all 85 bales are out – and the whole process takes less than 20 minutes. The bales are stacked two by two, again using forklift trucks, onto pallets. Within the hour, all are piled, safe and secure, in the dark, cool warehouse.

The raw cotton will stay here until it is hauled, on a sack-by-sack, as-and-when-needed basis, next door to the spinning and weaving sheds, where it will quickly be turned into thread.

Most of it will become top-quality pure cotton thread bound for the lucrative textile markets of Japan or the Middle East, while some of it may be weaved with polyester.

Either way, once it has left the storage shed and starts being transformed into thread, it will be back in a container bound for port within two weeks.

NYKU 596079–1, on the other hand, is heading back along the bumpy road to Surabaya port within minutes of being unloaded. Two hours later it is entering the Indra Jaya container yard, a few hundred meters from the port's main gates.

Facilities like Indra Jaya appear all over the world. Here, empty containers are checked on arrival for damage and are then washed. If necessary they are repaired or even fumigated and then stored, ready for the next trip to wherever in the world. It's a busy place.

All the major shipping companies rent space in Indra Jaya's vast lot – big enough to store 30,000 containers – and more than 300 boxes leave every day. The incessant movement – of trucks coming and going and containers being lifted up and down – makes the Earth shake.

A container's wait at Indra Jaya may be a day or may be a month – it all depends on local supply and demand. On this occasion, NYKU 596079–1 has to wait two days, after which it is pulled from the stack and sent light to Jakarta, more than 800 kilometers away to the west.

It's part of a batch of 30 empty containers sent across Java to help meet increased demand from two major global corporations that manufacture in the Greater Jakarta area.

So after another two days traveling along Java's dusty highways, NYKU 596079–1 once again enters a container yard and is ready for a wash.

Most of the
raw Californian cotton
that arrives in Surabaya
will leave as pure
top-quality thread,
bound for the lucrative
textile markets of Japan
or the Middle East.

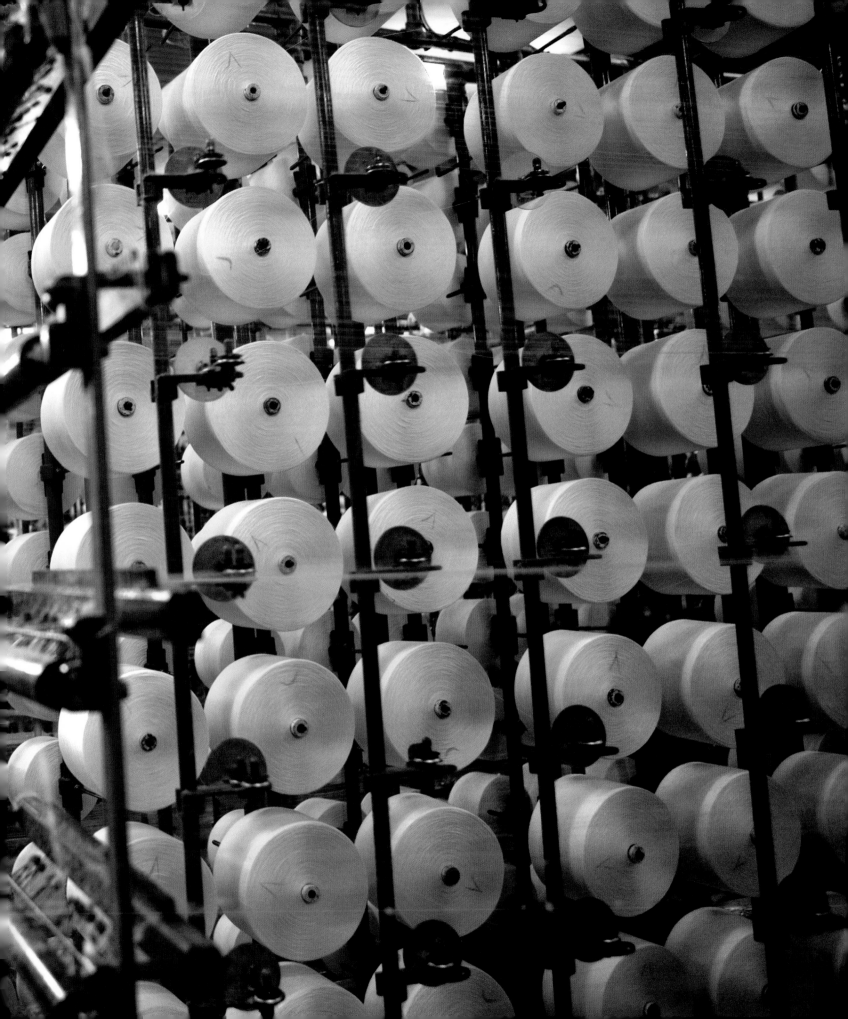

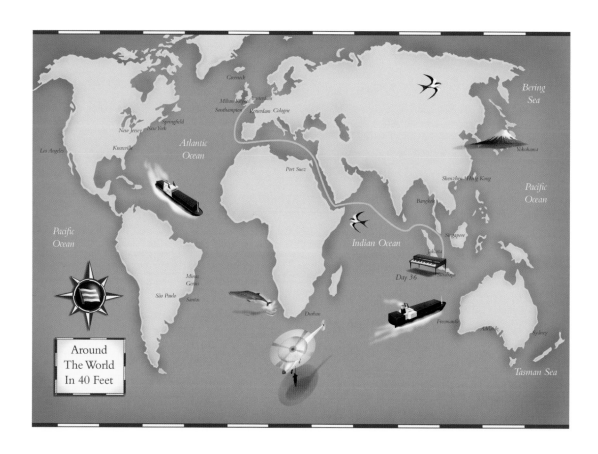

*Electric Pianos*
*Jakarta–Suez–Milton Keynes*

# Chapter 3

## DAY **30**, KILOMETER **25,814**
## JAKARTA, INDONESIA

The box now sits in Cikarang Barat, a modern, industrial yet well-manicured suburb 50 kilometers outside Jakarta. The area is a grid of smooth wide roads that sit in front of block after vast block of modern factories and warehouse complexes. Today, NYKU 596079–1 will take electric pianos to England.

The box was carried last night from an NYK container yard near the port in Jakarta and this morning was backed up to a loading bay alongside more than a dozen other NYK 40-foot containers. The piano manufacturer is a large multinational that is one of the world's biggest makers of musical instruments and NYK has a large-scale, multi-faceted global relationship with it. "This is one of our VIP clients," explains Tio Hendrik Hadiwijaya, General Manager, Marketing, NYK Line Indonesia, standing at the gate of the NYK yard watching the fleet of containers leave for the factory. "With customers like these, we try very hard to show them the scope of NYK's integrated network of logistics services and just how much more NYK can do for them."

Behind the loading bay where NYKU 596079–1 now sits is a sodium-lit warehouse filled with electronic musical instruments, all neatly boxed, packed immaculately on pallets and all displaying bar-coded information stickers detailing final destinations. Some pallets are bound for Australia, some for Belgium and some for Japan, while the tags on the pianos about to be loaded onto NYKU 596079–1 reveal their destination to be an NYK Logistics warehouse in Milton Keynes.

At the far end of the warehouse is a doorway that leads to a cavernous room that is home to the factory's six production lines. Here, one line is making tabletop electric pianos, another synthesizers and a third is handling huge electric grand pianos.

Each piece slowly but surely moves along its respective line toward the door and its export destiny: casings are worked

on first, microchips and circuit boards are added next, then keyboards are assembled. As each piece starts to look finished it is tested – and rising above the noise of drilling and high-pressure air jets is the surreal sound of repeated piano scales, in different tempos, tones and musical styles – before the instrument is boxed, stacked and sent on to the export warehouse.

The place is highly organized and impressive. Components, neatly arranged in racks and mobile shelving units, appear on the lines just as they are needed. Display boards above the workers' heads and at the end of each line reveal productivity rates, while also showing what product will come onto the line next, once the current batch is completed.

More than 3,000 people work here and each piano will take about five days to come through the system. Because the assembly line is one seamless row of ball bearing-supported racks and rollers, nothing is pushed or heaved; instead everything glides.

With the same efficiency and care shown on the lines inside, box NYKU 596079–1 is delicately loaded and leaves Cikarang Barat shortly after noon. It is caught in the horrendous afternoon traffic that is a much-detested daily hindrance to everyday life in Jakarta and arrives at the port at Tanjung Priok – a drive of less than 60 kilometers – four hours later.

NYKU 596079–1 will leave Jakarta on the Kaido tomorrow night, just before dusk. The ship is tiny in comparison with the intercontinental container ships. It is just 119 meters long, as opposed to 300 meters-plus for many of the bigger vessels in the NYK fleet, and has a capacity of just 550 TEUs, compared with more than 6,000 for the larger ships. Yet it, and hundreds of "feeder" vessels like it, plays a vital role in today's rapid door-to-door transport network.

The Kaido works a 2,000-kilometer, north-south axis shuttling between Jakarta in Indonesia, Port Kelang in Malaysia, Laem Chabang, on the coast outside Bangkok in Thailand and Singapore. Its run is short and its turnaround time, because of its small size, is also short – meaning it is very effective in sweeping up containers from the smaller ports in the manufacturing hubs across Southeast Asia and moving them quickly to the main shipping hubs, in this case Singapore.

Two days after leaving the piano factory, the box is on the quay at Singapore. Forty hours after that it is being picked up and placed in the cargo hold of the NYK Aquarius. And the following morning it is heading northwest toward the Malacca Straits, Colombo, the Suez Canal and finally Europe.

**OPPOSITE PAGE –** Box NYKU 596079–1 leaves Jakarta on the Kaido, a small yet swift "feeder" vessel that works a 2,000-kilometer "Singapore swing", connecting ports in Indonesia and Malaysia in the south and Thailand in the north.

**ABOVE –** The Kaido is tiny in comparison with today's modern intercontinental container ships. Yet its run is short and its turnarounds are quick, making it – and hundreds of ships like it – indispensable in today's world of rapid door-to-door transport.

Two days after leaving
the piano factory
in Indonesia, the
box is on the quay
at Singapore. Forty
hours after that it is
in the cargo hold of
the NYK Aquarius
and the following
morning it is heading
toward the Malacca
Straits, Colombo,
the Suez Canal and
finally Europe.

## DAY **49**, KILOMETER **34,947**
## PORT SUEZ, EGYPT

G amal Mazhar stares intently out across the
choppy, inky black sea, mutters quietly in Arabic
and looks down at a faxed copy of an anchorage
chart that he has pulled from his jacket pocket.
He peers again through the sea-splashed glass and then
points to a twinkling set of lights away in the distance, and nods
to the captain of the launch.

A few moments later, Gamal pulls a radio receiver down
from above his head and says, in slow, deliberate English, "NYK
Aquarius, NYK Aquarius, this is ship's agent Port Suez. Do you
copy, Aquarius?"

There is static silence on the radio as the launch carrying
Gamal across the northwestern tip of the Red Sea continues to
bounce through the wind-blown waves. He looks again at his
chart, then back out to the sea and the lights.

"This is NYK Aquarius," squawks the radio in reply. "Ship's
agent, Port Suez. Aquarius copies you, over." Gamal smiles.
"Good evening, Aquarius. I will show you my light. Please, tell
me when you see me, Aquarius." And with that the skipper
flashes the floodlight on the roof of the launch's tiny cabin, on
and off, on and off, for 20 seconds, until the reply comes: "I see
you, my friend. I see you."

After a few more brief radio exchanges between two
parties that have clearly done this many times before, the NYK
Aquarius lowers its gangplank and Gamal, despite the wind-
driven swell and the large wad of documents under his arm,
deftly hops from his tiny vessel to a much bigger one.

It's almost midnight and the Aquarius has been at anchor
for three hours, waiting to enter the southern end of the
Suez Canal. Access to the canal is strictly controlled and
all ships entering have to complete a raft of formalities – hence
Gamal's wad of documents – and operate within a strict set of
transit rules. Ships travel in single file through the 163-kilometer

canal and do so in three daily convoys: two southbound convoys depart each morning from Port Said on the Mediterranean Sea and a northbound convoy departs from Port Suez, on the Red Sea.

The ships cross each other at two lakes – the Little Bitter Lake and the Great Bitter Lake – near the canal's middle, where one convoy stops at anchor to allow the other to pass. More than 100 ships might transit in a day and the whole process is an elaborate, carefully orchestrated – and expensive – ritual that occurs on every day of the year.

Within 30 minutes Gamal has completed his form-filling tasks and he bids farewell to the Aquarius, re-boards his launch and heads back to Egyptian soil and his bed. Meanwhile, up on the bridge, the ship's second officer, Sayoto Gil, is just settling into his regular midnight to 04.00 watch shift.

At 03.53 he receives a VHF radio call from Suez Port control, informing the Aquarius of its position in tomorrow's 23-ship northbound convoy. The Aquarius will be Number 3 in the queue, near the convoy's front, which means a lively start for the crew. Within the hour, Captain Nikola Tabar is on the bridge.

The captain strides across his domain and as he does so, he takes in the ship's log and the waters around him – by glancing at the bridge's long bank of blinking screens and by using his binoculars – and then strolls out onto the starboard bridge wing to take in the slightly chilly early-morning breeze.

It's a beautiful scene: the sun is beginning to inch its way over the mountains far behind the Sinai Desert to the east. As it does so, its rays hit the golden roof of a mosque sitting on the canal's western bank, while in the mouth of the waterway a pod of dolphins briefly appears, breaking the surface in graceful unison half a dozen times before disappearing beneath the aquamarine waves.

Tabar, who says he has been at sea "for a very long time", quietly takes in the scene for a brief moment before pacing back onto the bridge. With one quick-fire sentence he gives the order for the ship to depart, enquires about the status of the pilot who will shortly be coming aboard and orders a pot of freshly brewed coffee from the galley. "And please," he says, "make it strong," as he surveys the rapidly brightening sea ahead of him. Captain Tabar knows from experience that this will be a long day.

By sundown, the Aquarius – and box NYKU 596079–1 – will be in the Mediterranean.

**ABOVE –** On the Suez Canal, Chief Officer Stanko Delic oversees the lowering of NYK Aquarius' anchor as the ship pauses on the Great Bitter Lake, one of the 163-kilometer canal's two purpose-built passing places.

**OPPOSITE PAGE –** As is the convention in confined and crowded waters, a sequence of Egyptian marine pilots (top) joins the NYK Aquarius as it transits the Suez Canal. On "up" journeys the first pilot joins at the canal's southern entrance at Port Suez, the second joins for the middle section and the last, as the ship approaches the Mediterranean Sea, at Port Said.

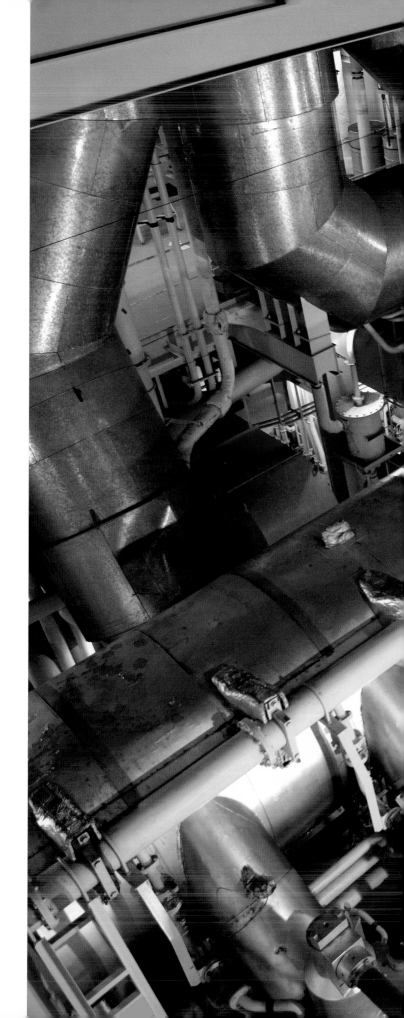

## DAY 50, KILOMETER 35,011
# GREAT BITTER LAKE, EGYPT

There's a delay at the Great Bitter Lake. The anchorage time here is normally little more than one hour but already the Aquarius has been sitting for two – and still more ships keep appearing from the canal to the north, looking on the horizon like huge unworldly beasts slowly gliding across the sand.

Next to Captain Tabar on the bridge is an Egyptian pilot, who is using the delay to take a breakfast of eggs, cheese, toast and honey. He is the second of three pilots who will help guide the ship through the canal's various sections. Every port has its own pilots who are local experts. They join vessels – sometimes for an hour, sometimes for a few days – and work alongside ships' deck officers to guide ships in or out safely.

The pilot pauses during his breakfast to listen in to the unremitting Arabic radio chat among the dozens of other pilots working on the canal, then informs the captain that in the approaching convoy are three very large vessels that, understandably, are taking their time. The captain looks at his watch once again, sighs, stares at the sand dunes all around and then goes downstairs to resume his own breakfast.

Traveling along the Suez Canal is a surreal experience. The landscape is largely featureless: there are oil pipelines, the odd dusty road, the occasional military compound or tented settlement and sometimes small clusters of palm trees, but mainly it is just sand dunes, stretching from canal shore to horizon. However, for Captain Tabar and his crew, made up of Croatians (including Tabar), Filipinos and a Slovenian, it is just another day at work. The Aquarius' current schedule has the ship on a 56-day, 13-port run from Yokohama to Hamburg and takes it twice through the Suez on each loop… and is therefore nothing out of the ordinary.

When at sea, the crew work eight-hour days, normally split into two shifts of four hours, while in port they work rotas of

six hours on, six hours off. They remain on board for three to nine months, depending on their contracts. Although the ship is immaculately clean and modern – everyone has private cabins and there is basketball, ping-pong, a gym, an outside barbecue and communal video areas on board – today's container ship is ultimately a utilitarian and deadly serious place. The crew all quickly acknowledge they are here for work and when asked what they miss most while at sea, the reply is always the same: "family". However, despite the disciplined environment, the vessel retains a friendly yet dignified atmosphere and, in long-standing maritime tradition, all guests are treated warmly.

At the ship's physical and metaphorical heart is the engine room. Tended by 10 men, it is home to a sewage treatment plant, a garbage incinerator, four 3,000-kilowatt generators and a gargantuan 12-cylinder engine, which gives the Aquarius a range of 40,000 kilometers. The bridge, the hi-tech brain of the ship, is run by four officers, who on this trip are assisted by three cadets, while the soul of the ship – the galley and the two messes (one for officers and one for ratings) – has a staff of three. One of the pluses of the ship's transcontinental route is that Chief Cook Rico Dino gets to use the world as his own private supermarket. "We buy our fish in Singapore, our fresh vegetables in Suez and our meat in Germany. We can get the best of everything," he says. The crew undoubtedly eat well here: tonight the Europeans are eating fish soup followed by goulash served with polenta, while the Filipinos enjoy fresh fried fish, stewed chicken and steamed rice. Rico says catering is something the captain plays close attention to. "It's important," confirms Tabar. "This is our home."

Up on the bridge, the pilot has finished his breakfast and the Aquarius is once again moving north. The delay has left Captain Tabar unconcerned. "We will easily make up the time running up to Southampton," he says. This run north will be Tabar's last on the Aquarius. At Hamburg, his contract finishes and he will return home to Croatia and, after six months at sea, he is clearly looking forward to it.

There are two westward sea lanes through the Mediterranean and Captain Tabar plans to take the more northerly one. It cuts across the bottom of Crete and Sicily and therefore takes the ship close to the Adriatic Sea and Croatia. And, before sundown, the Aquarius approaches the mouth of the canal and the sandy Egyptian shoreline that has been gliding by all day starts to fade. Captain Tabar stands out on the bridge wings once more and looks north. "I taste the Mediterranean," he says with a smile.

**ABOVE –** Captain Nikola Tabar (center), who says he has been at sea "for a very long time", consults the Aquarius' sophisticated electronic navigational systems with two of his deck officers.

**OPPOSITE PAGE –** As dusk begins to descend across the dunes that surround the Suez Canal, Captain Tabar checks the ship's planned passage out of the northern end of the canal at Port Said and on through the Mediterranean.

## DAY **56**, KILOMETER **40,995**
## SOUTHAMPTON, ENGLAND

After six days on the open sea, the NYK Aquarius approaches the Port of Southampton. As it does so, a jet-skier moves in close and thinks about riding its swirling, foaming wake. "Maniac," says Hugh McCormack, the skipper of the Surrey, one of two tugs that are bringing the Aquarius in on this blustery morning. The jet-skier approaches, glances up at the ship that towers way above him and then pulls away, making Hugh laugh with disdain.

Hugh, or "Twinkle" as he is known, has been working aboard Southampton tugs for more than 40 years and says he started at the age of 15. "You were meant to be 16, but I lied," he says with a roguish, toothy grin.

He says the work then was all mechanical and needed a crew of eight. Now, with its high-powered electric winches, the Surrey needs a crew of just three.

"It's not really the same job," says Hugh as he gracefully pulls his craft alongside the stern of the Aquarius so the tug crew can catch the ship's lead ropes and secure them to the tug's own thick lines, which the deck hands aboard the Aquarius in turn winch back up and fasten.

Once the tug is secure, Hugh stays in constant contact, via radio, with the Southampton pilot who is up on the bridge of the Aquarius, working alongside Captain Tabar.

The teams operate in synchronicity and make their work look straightforward, which it clearly is not. They have to place this 300-meter vessel between two fixed marks and have to do so with less than half a meter's leeway either side. The dredged channel they are in is 60 meters wide, the ship is 40 meters wide and there is a strong easterly wind that constantly blows ship and tug toward the shore.

"Actually, the easterly is not too bad," says Hugh with a dismissive shake of his head. "When the westerly blows, it

moves the ship away from the channel and then things can get tricky," he adds, nursing his tea in one hand and the helm of the tug – which is pulling the 60,000 tonne Aquarius – with the other.

"In truth, we don't do most of the work. If you have a good pilot like him up there," he says, waving his tea mug in the general direction of the Aquarius' bridge, "then we are only really here as backup."

At 09.27 the ship docks – to the exact half-meter and three minutes ahead of schedule – and before the gangway has touched the quay the port's cranes are moving into position.

The Aquarius will deliver 1,146 containers onto the quay – including box NYKU 596079–1, with its Indonesian electric pianos – and will pick up 986 in return. It is scheduled to be in port for just 22 hours, which leaves very little time for rest and relaxation.

Captain Tabar reckons that although the ship has a capacity of 6,252 TEUs, more than 18,000 containers are moved in or out of its eight vast cargo bays during every 56-day loop, meaning smooth port turnarounds are vital to the ship's operational success.

Which is why, as soon as the gangway is down, Chief Officer Stanko Delic takes a seat in the ship's office on A deck with Geoff Bowers, from NYK Port Operations, Southampton, to run through the Aquarius' load plan.

The load plan is like a constantly updated electronic relay baton that is passed from port to port. As soon as the Aquarius left Suez and entered the Mediterranean, box NYKU 596079–1, together with all the other boxes on board, became the responsibility of a ship planner in NYK Europe's head office in London.

He has received an electronic file from the last port of call – in this case Singapore – which he updates and sends on to each port of call in Europe. These ports then add their own load data to the file, which is then passed to the ship, the local NYK office and the port's terminal team.

When the process is finished, a new file is sent on to the next port – in this case Amsterdam – and the whole process starts again.

Box NYKU 596079–1 was one of the last boxes to be loaded at Singapore, for the simple reason that it is coming off at the next port of call. By midday the box is on English soil; before evening it is out of the port and on the move once again, moving north… through driving rain.

## DAY **57**, KILOMETER **41,131**
# MILTON KEYNES, ENGLAND

John Rushbridge looks out of his cab window at the dark English sky above and scowls. "There's more rain coming," he says. John is a truck driver on a full-time contract with NYK Logistics. On this damp morning he is sitting in a warehouse compound in central England, waiting to be given the go-ahead to back up NYKU 596079–1 to a loading bay to be emptied.

John picked the box up yesterday afternoon at Southampton port, drove 150 kilometers north, and then spent the night in his cab – and behind the guarded gates – at the warehouse on the edge of Milton Keynes. Once it is emptied, he will take the box to a container yard next to the NYK Logistics Distribution Center in Northampton, 30 kilometers to the north of here, where he will have a shower, eat breakfast and be told where his next job will take him.

His cab is a veritable home-from-home and boasts a full-sized, comfortable bed, a fridge, a kettle, a TV and a laptop computer connected to the Internet. "I spend a lot of time in here," says John. "It needs to be nice."

He has been driving trucks since the 1970s and although he used to drive all over Europe and beyond, nowadays he prefers to stay closer to home. His week normally starts with his picking up a container at Southampton port; his work can then take him on a string of containers drops and pick-ups across the UK – perhaps to a warehouse, then another port, or back to Southampton and then to a warehouse again. "For five days I live in here and keep moving, then on Friday I go home to my wife," he says.

At just before 08.00 John is given the signal and he swings his truck back against bay Number 4. Within seconds the box's two plastic seals are cut, the doors are swung open and the inside of box NYKU 596079–1 sees daylight for the first time in 21 days – after a journey of more than 13,000 kilometers

involving two ships, two trucks and three ports. Then, with oft-demonstrated expertise, a forklift truck driver starts to lift the bulky electric pianos carefully from the box and into the pristinely ordered stacks that line the warehouse.

The facility is managed by NYK. For more than a decade, NYK Logistics has run all aspects of the warehouse's operations on behalf of the instrument manufacturer. They oversee all inbound deliveries, look after all inventory and stock-handling matters and also provide a freight-forwarding service that moves the instruments across the UK and continental Europe.

Stuart Baren, Contract Manager, NYK Logistics, the man responsible for the day-to-day running of the warehouse, watches the container being unloaded as he explains how the system operates. "NYK work as closely as we can with the customer. The customer handles ordering, sales and the technical matters – like tuning the instruments when they arrive, or helping with home installations – while we handle just about everything else."

Stuart reckons that more than 75% of the instruments that come here are pre-ordered. "This means we just store most goods overnight. We receive about five containers a day, from either Southampton or Felixstowe, which have come directly from the customer's factories in China, Indonesia or Japan, and we will have the majority of the goods ready to go out the next day," he adds.

The goods, says Stuart, are delivered by one of three methods: they are grouped together into mixed orders and sent to stores across the UK via one of four nationwide NYK Logistics Centers; or they are sent individually, via a domestic courier service, straight into homes; or they are sent directly as one-product bulk orders to key stores, which is exactly what will happen to the electric pianos from Indonesia.

Within 48 hours – and less than a month after being on a production line on the other side of the world – the pianos from NYKU 596079–1 will be on display and ready for sale in a central London music store. "Our job is to make sure this process happens as smoothly as possible," concludes Stuart, as the last of the pianos is plucked from the box.

By 09.00, all the pianos are safely stored and John Rushbridge is preparing to take NYKU 596079–1 from Milton Keynes to Northampton. By lunchtime, he is pulling another container towards Felixstowe and by 15.00, an empty NYKU 596079–1 is on the back of another truck and heading north once more, this time to Scotland.

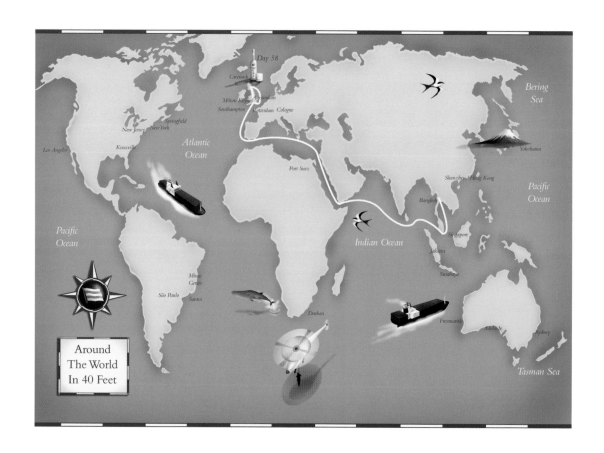

*Whisky*
*Greenock–Southampton–Bangkok*

# Chapter 4

## DAY **58**, KILOMETER **41,755**
# GREENOCK, SCOTLAND

Box NYKU 596079–1 sits in a stack of four containers on a wind-swept dock at Clydeport, in Greenock, about 40 kilometers outside the city of Glasgow. It has been in Scotland for only 48 hours but already it is about to leave again, aboard the feeder vessel Sea Vita, which crosses the Irish Sea to and from the "Celtic triangle" ports of Liverpool, Belfast and Greenock, before heading south down to England and Southampton.

Greenock is one of the few export-orientated ports in the UK and the Sea Vita mainly picks up empty containers from the more import-orientated ports of Liverpool and Belfast and moves them to Greenock, where they go to various sites around Scotland to be filled.

"And it's nearly always with whisky," says Hugh Hardie, who, as Assistant Operations Manager at Clydeport, is overseeing today's loading process. "Ninety percent of these boxes," he says, waving his left hand in a sweep across the container-dotted dock, "are filled with the stuff."

Clydeport was built in the 1960s with the intention of it being a Western Scottish gateway to North America, although, as Hugh explains, it is now solely a container feeder port that receives five to 10 smallish container vessels a week that are filled here – mainly with whisky – and taken to the far bigger ports of Southampton and Rotterdam.

From there, this much-loved Scottish export goes mostly to Asia, with significant amounts also ending up in North America and in the tourist playgrounds of southern Spain and Portugal.

The dockyards along the Clyde Estuary were, for more than a century, home to one of the busiest shipbuilding areas in the world, and as such played a seminal role in the development of global shipping. However, by the 1980s, the industry had all but died out and the ensuing economic

shortfall was devastating. Matters, thankfully, are much better now, and part of the turnaround is, as Hugh points out, down to the millions of cases of whisky that leave Scotland's shores every year.

Box NYKU 596079–1 is also filled with whisky… almost 20,000 bottles of 12-year-old blended Scotch sit snugly inside in shrink-wrapped palletized boxes. The container arrived in Scotland empty two nights ago and sat in a sprawling container park in the western suburbs of Glasgow before being moved, as part of a much bigger fleet of NYK 40-foot containers, to a large-scale distillery-cum-bottling plant complex in Paisley, again on the western fringes of Glasgow.

The facility is, in every sense of the word, huge. It receives a relentless stream of tankers that bring both blended and unblended Scotch from a network of other distilleries and blending houses across the Scottish Highlands.

The tankers line up before plugging into any one of 10 bottling lines that, combined, handle more than 10 million cases a year. At the other end of the operation, once bottled, the spirit is swiftly packed for travel and loaded aboard the waiting line of container trucks lining up to whisk the whisky to Clydeport, 30 minutes down the road, or to the freight rail terminal at Moss Head, about the same distance in the other direction. More than 80 containers leave the site every day.

The whisky inside box NYKU 596079–1 is heading to Thailand. It will first spend two days aboard the Sea Vita as it heads down the Irish Sea and then along the English Channel to Southampton, where the box will spend another day on the quay. Then it will be loaded aboard the NYK Lyra and will travel back the same way it came five days ago on the Aquarius: past Gibraltar and through the Mediterranean, back through the Suez Canal and the Indian Ocean and back into the transhipment area at Singapore port.

After a day there it will be transferred to another feeder vessel, the ACX Tsubaki, which shuttles back and forth on the 1,300-kilometer north-south Gulf of Thailand route and will reach Laem Chabang port 12 days after leaving Scotland.

As the last of the boxes is swung aboard the Sea Vita, Hugh Hardie chuckles. "These metal boxes get to travel the world while I," he says as he points at the high dark dock cranes and the black storm clouds gathering above them, "get to come back here, every day." He laughs again. "It doesn't seem fair, does it?"

**ABOVE –** Box NYKU 596079–1 leaves Scottish soil at Clydeport, about 40 kilometers outside the city of Glasgow. It is one of the UK's few export ports thanks to the huge worldwide demand for Scotch whisky.

**OPPOSITE PAGE –** The box spends less than 48 hours in Scotland – which is time enough to be filled with almost 20,000 bottles of 12-year-old blended Scotch. From Scotland the whisky will go, via Southampton and Singapore, to Bangkok, Thailand.

The box arrived at Laem Chabang and then traveled by train to NYK's Inland Container Depot at Lat Krabang, on the Thai capital's sprawling eastern fringe. Here, the whisky is unloaded and will wait, in storage, until the customer is ready to distribute it to a network of bars, hotels and shops across greater Bangkok and beyond.

**ABOVE –** The whisky takes 12 long years to mature… but less than a month to move from Scottish distillery to downtown Bangkok bar top.

**OPPOSITE PAGE –** Once the whisky is unloaded, box NYKU 596079–1 is on the move again, heading through Bangkok's heat to another warehouse complex, where it picks up a consignment of microwave ovens bound for Australia.

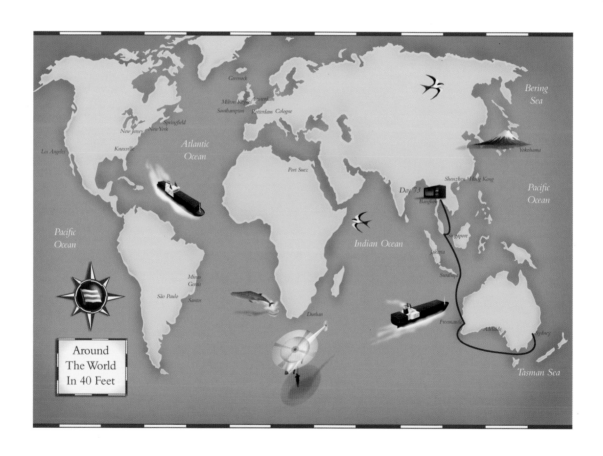

*Microwave Ovens*
*Bangkok–Laem Chabang–Sydney*

# Chapter 5

## DAY **73**, KILOMETER **56,594**
# LAEM CHABANG, THAILAND

I t's a fiercely hot afternoon in Thailand. Between container moves, the stevedores working on the decks of the NYK Atlas try to find time to scurry beneath the bulkheads in search of a few seconds' shade. The ship's thermometer is showing 39 degrees Celsius (102 degrees Fahrenheit). It's warm, even by Thai standards.

Twenty meters above, up on the bridge of the ship, where the window blinds and air-conditioning are just about keeping the tropical sun at bay, Junior Third Officer Aya Yoshioka is quietly studying the ship's charts. Aya has been with NYK for only five months and apart from being the youngest crew member aboard the Atlas, Aya is something of a maritime rarity… because she is female.

The Atlas, a two-year-old, state-of-the-art ship, has just left dry dock and will leave Thailand today to start a 42-day service that takes in Singapore, Kaohsiung, Los Angeles, Tokyo and Shekou. Aya has never made the notorious North Pacific crossing before, or visited the United States. And she readily admits she is apprehensive yet excited about the prospect. "It was my childhood dream to travel the seas and…" she says with a warm, slightly self-conscious smile, "here I am."

The ship, together with box NYKU 596079–1, is in Laem Chabang, Thailand's main port, about 110 kilometers south of Bangkok; the box has had another whirlwind turnaround, spending less than four days on Thai soil.

It arrived from Singapore at Laem Chabang, then traveled by train to NYK's Inland Container Depot at Lat Krabang, on the Thai capital's sprawling eastern fringe. There, the Scotch whisky was unloaded and will wait, in storage, until the customer is ready to distribute it to a network of bars, hotels and shops across greater Bangkok and beyond.

Empty, the box spent one more night at the Lat Krabang yard before traveling to an assembly-line complex to the south

of Bangkok, where it was filled once more – this time with microwave ovens destined for Australia.

The complex – which produces home consumer appliances for markets worldwide – is also home to an NYK Export Service Center that handles all the site's shipping needs. It's a busy place: the center packs anything from 40 to 100 containers a day and, within two hours of arriving at the site, NYKU 596079–1 is filled and moving once again, back to the port at Laem Chabang, to be loaded aboard the Atlas.

The box will travel with the ship for only 1,300 kilometers, then spend time in the familiar transshipment stacks at Singapore port before transferring to another vessel, the NYK Kamakura, which will take it south.

It will then travel across the Java Sea before heading through the Selat Sunda Channel, between the Indonesian islands of Java and Sumatra, and continue south along the eastern edge of the Indian Ocean to Australia.

It will stop briefly at the western Australian port of Fremantle before traveling east across the Great Australian Bight, past Tasmania to Sydney, where the microwave ovens will be off-loaded at an out-of-town distribution center. The 7,500-kilometer journey aboard the Kamakura from Singapore to Sydney will take 11 days, while the 1,300-kilometer scoot across the Gulf of Thailand, which Third Officer Aya Yoshioka is meticulously mapping on the bridge of the Atlas, will last just 72 hours.

The captain of the Atlas, Takuzo Okada, watches over Aya as she works. In contrast to his Junior Third Officer, the captain has been with NYK since 1977. But, just like Aya, it was his childhood dream to take to the high seas, and despite having been a sailor for almost three decades, he still loves the life. "I have done various stints on shore. It is the NYK way, to get people to learn other sides of the business," he says. "I have worked as a ship's agent and in portside container relocation, but when I do, I really miss the sea."

Captain Okada says he welcomes the fact that more female names are beginning to appear on ships' crew lists. "Why not?" he asks. "Aya is smart and will make a very good officer, and I hope a very good captain one day. I know this: she's smarter than I was at her age."

And with that, he leaves Junior Third Officer Aya Yoshioka in peace to finish mapping the course for a vessel, at a dead weight of 81,171 tonnes, which will, after leaving port this evening, head into some of the busiest sea lanes in the world.

**OPPOSITE PAGE –** The microwave ovens loaded in Bangkok will be carried aboard the NYK Atlas as far as Singapore, where ship and box part company: the Atlas heads east to America, while NYKU 596079–1 heads south, aboard the Kamakura, to Australia.

**ABOVE –** Aboard the NYK Atlas, veteran Captain Takuzo Okada runs through the ship's passage plan with Junior Third Officer Aya Yoshioka, who will soon make her first trip across the notoriously rough North Pacific.

The box travels across the Java Sea before heading through the Selat Sunda Channel, between the Indonesian islands of Java and Sumatra, and continuing south along the eastern edge of the Indian Ocean to Australia. It stops briefly at the Western Australian port of Fremantle before traveling east across the Great Australian Bight to Sydney.

**ABOVE** – The box lands at Port Botany in Sydney aboard the Kamakura, after an arduous schedule that has seen it travel by train, truck and no fewer than seven ships, and cover more than 40,000 kilometers in less than 50 days.

**OPPOSITE PAGE** – In Australia the box slows down. After dropping off the microwave ovens at a warehouse in the east of the city, it will wait for a week in storage at a railhead container yard before traveling by train across southern Australia to Adelaide, covering a mere 1,100 kilometers in 30 days.

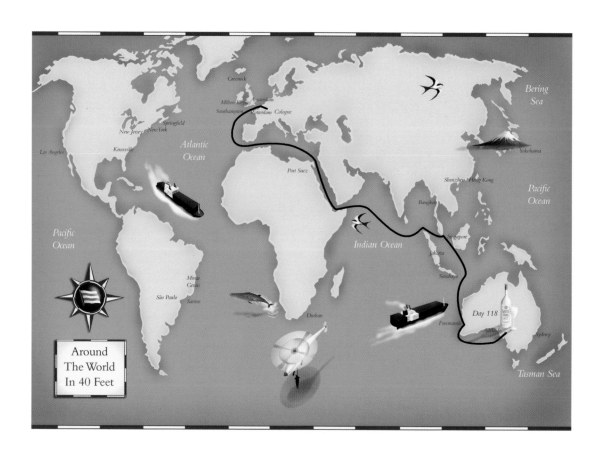

*White Wine*
*Adelaide–Singapore–Amsterdam*

# Chapter 6

## DAY **118**, KILOMETER **66,398**
# ADELAIDE, AUSTRALIA

The box has slowed down. It arrived in Australia 30 days ago aboard the Kamakura, landing at Botany Bay, the same bay in which Captain James Cook first landed Down Under 237 years ago. From there, box NYKU 596079–1 was carried 30 kilometers across town to a cavernous distribution warehouse in Huntingwood, on the city's eastern edge. Here the microwave ovens were unloaded; and in finest just-in-time style, they were sent out the next day to stores across Sydney to fulfil existing stock orders. The box, meanwhile, moved back across the city to Cooks River Container Yard, where it was placed in a storage stack, waiting to be repositioned for its next job.

Like so many of the world's more affluent cities, Sydney imports far more than it exports, meaning a lot of boxes are moved empty – either within Australia, or back north to the manufacturing hubs in Asia – to find their next cargos.

Cooks River Container Yard was purposely built around an important railhead that serves all Australia, and so, after waiting six days at the yard, box NYKU 596079–1 was loaded aboard a container freight train, the 3103 Aboriginal Stockman. Along with 29 other forty-foot containers, it was then carried 1,100 kilometers west, across New South Wales and into South Australia, where it was placed in McKenzie's Container Yard, another rail head facility, this time right next to Adelaide port.

Although Adelaide is a small port, it sits in the center of a richly fertile stretch of coastline and, as such, is a thriving export port that moves significant amounts of cotton, grain and fish feed (for the tuna farms in Tasmania), as well as wine – the area's most important export – and, intriguingly, premium-quality hay that is moved to the Middle East and into some of the world's finest stables, where it is used as feed for racehorses and racing camels.

Box NYKU 596079–1 is in Adelaide to be loaded with wine – 28,224 bottles of Chardonnay, which will end up on supermarket shelves in The Netherlands. Between the container yard and the port is the loading center for one of the oldest and biggest winemakers in Australia. The winemaker used to take the containers to be loaded at its main bottling plant, two hours outside Adelaide. Now, in a smoother, integrated loading system, the wine is brought by smaller domestic trucks to the loading center, where it is loaded into the waiting export containers, cleared by customs and then driven, just a few meters, into the back gate of the port. Like the microwave ovens that were sold to stores across Sydney before they left the production line in Thailand, most of the wine that comes through Adelaide has buyers – in this case, one of The Netherlands' largest supermarket chains – before it has left its bottling line.

However, before NYKU 596079–1 can be filled with wine, it must first pass a "cleanliness" test. All NYK containers, wherever they are in the world, are constantly assessed and graded according to condition. Only those with "A" grades (the cleanest) are deemed fit to carry products for human consumption. Because of the large numbers of food products that are shipped out of Adelaide, the McKenzie staff, on behalf of NYK, run a strict inspection system for all the containers that come into their yard. So, when box NYKU 596079–1 is swung from the back of the Aboriginal Stockman into the yard, it first goes through a visual inspection – by sight and by smell – to check that the container is structurally sound, before receiving a more thorough examination to ensure the interior is good enough to carry food products. After its travels, the box's exterior is a tad grubby but the inside – the important part – is deemed acceptable. After an exterior wash and a rigorous high-pressure steam clean, the box is ready for the wine.

The distance from container yard to loading center to port stacks covers less than a kilometer and the whole loading process takes less than a working day. And once the box is filled, waiting for it at the port is the NYK Kamakura, the same ship that took it down to Sydney from Singapore.

Since NYKU 596079–1 arrived in Australia, it has traveled about 1,300 kilometers. The Kamakura, on the other hand, has completed a whole 14,000-odd kilometer loop of its 28-day service, which extends from Port Kelang in Malaysia to Sydney and takes in Singapore, Fremantle, Melbourne and Adelaide – meaning it is ready to take NYKU 596079–1 back on board to start another journey north to Singapore, Suez and Europe.

When box NYKU 596079–1 is swung from the back of the Aboriginal Stockman into the Adelaide yard, it first goes through a thorough examination to ensure the interior is good enough to carry food products… and after an exterior wash and a rigorous high–pressure steam clean, the box is declared fit to carry wine.

**OPPOSITE PAGE –** Box NYKU 596079–1 leaves Australia at Adelaide, a small yet significant port that sits at the heart of a richly fertile stretch of coastline and exports sizeable quantities of wine, wheat and wool.

**LEFT –** At a port-side loading center (bottom) at Port Adelaide, the box is loaded with 28,224 bottles of Chardonnay. Domestic trailers carry the wine to the port from a state-of-the art bottling plant outside the city that serves a large area of South Australia, one of the country's most important wine-producing regions.

## DAY **131**, KILOMETER **72,099**
# TANJONG PAGAR, SINGAPORE

In Singapore, it is approaching 14.00 and raining. It's dark with heavy, typically loud tropical rain – the sort of stuff that renders even the best wet-weather gear hopeless in a matter of minutes. The downpour has not relented for three hours and, across the city, the drains have turned to torrents and the lunchtime traffic is beginning to back up in the drenched downtown streets.

At the port, however, operations continue as usual, as NYKU 596079–1 is lifted from the back of a terminal truck, up through the deluge, and onto the rain-lashed deck of the NYK Lynx.

NYKU 596079–1 arrived here on the Kamakura at 03.00 and is going aboard the Lynx, due to depart from Singapore at 17.50 today; it will leave the ship at the Ceres Paragon Terminal, Amsterdam.

The fact that the box is back at Singapore, or indeed that it's the box's fifth visit to the city in four months, despite never having actually picked up or unloaded a cargo here, should not really come as a surprise, because Singapore, more than any other port, is the world's maritime crossroads.

The port handles more than 24 million TEUs a year and 80% of them are – just like NYKU 596079–1 – transhipment cargos that never leave the confines of the port. Instead they are placed in temporary storage, in impressively high stacks of eight, before being whisked off by another crane, to another ship and another destination.

It's a system that is automated, quick and one that must be very efficient because, amazingly, more than 20% of all of the world's container cargo passes through this port.

It is also a system that requires a lot of space. Unlike a lot of modern ports that are situated well away from the city, most of the port terminals in Singapore are close to the center. Which means the towering storage stacks – in enough

space for more than 200,000 containers – at times seem to envelop this most compact of cities.

"This is part of the reason why so many of the world's warehouses are now empty," says Alex Chan, NYK Line Asia's Assistant Manager, Operations, pointing to the rows of stacks. "It is this sort of transhipment system that allows just-in-time principles to really work, with this," he says, pointing again to row upon row of immaculately lined-up container stacks, "acting as some kind of high-speed global warehouse."

Alex explains that NYK can move a container through Singapore quicker than through any other port in the world. "We used to need 24 hours. If you didn't get the box into port 24 hours before the next vessel was leaving, you missed the cut-off and had to wait for the next ship," he says. "Then, a few years ago, it was brought down to 12 hours and then to two hours and actually, nowadays, the port can do it in just an hour. It's what we call a premium connection."

This means that within an hour of one ship arriving and another departing, the box's electronic packet of information, which includes its own NYK booking reference number, plus its own bill of lading – stating where it came from, where it is going to, what it is carrying and for whom – together with its own customs authenticity number, must be processed, cleared, dispatched and checked before the box can be whisked through the maze of metal to the correct departing vessel.

Mistakes, says Alex, are very uncommon. "If you say you can do it all very quickly and then start losing boxes, well then there's no point, is there?" Currently Alex says NYK moves about 1.2 million boxes through Singapore, 90% of which are carrying transhipment cargos and 6% of which are "premium" one-hour connections.

"There are so many ship connections from here, and the turnaround time is now so short, that people know they can put things through Singapore and cut it really fine and it will work out."

Today, NYKU 596079–1 does not need one of Singapore's specialty high-speed connections because it has 13 hours' transit time, which is close to eternity in the rapidly moving Lion City.

It is swung onto the deck of the Lynx – one of 1,382 containers that are taken onboard in less than 12 hours – and by nightfall the rain has stopped and box NYKU 596079–1 is moving once again, north through the Malacca Straits, bound for Europe.

**LEFT –** Alex Chan, NYK Line Asia's Assistant Manager, Operations (top), explains how Singapore port handles more than 24 million container units a year and how 80% of them – just like NYKU 596079–1 – hold transhipment cargos that never leave the confines of the port.

**OPPOSITE PAGE –** Despite the torrential rain, work goes on at the Port of Singapore. Throughout the storm, container-loading operations continue; once the rain has passed, the NYK Lynx takes on fuel from a "bunker tanker" that comes alongside the ship.

The NYK Lynx took on two pilots outside Amsterdam who, as the 40-meter-wide ship painstakingly crept along the series of narrow sea locks, stood on each bridge wing monitoring the portable GPS units that all Dutch pilots use to carry out this tight, tricky work.

**OPPOSITE PAGE –** The box lands in Europe at NYK's Ceres Paragon Terminal, outside Amsterdam. Its immense overhead loading cranes that span both sides of the U-shaped dock make it one of the fastest-working terminals in the world.

**ABOVE –** The Chardonnay from NYKU 596079–1, after traveling almost 20,000 kilometers, is on shop shelves across The Netherlands within a month of leaving the Adelaide winery.

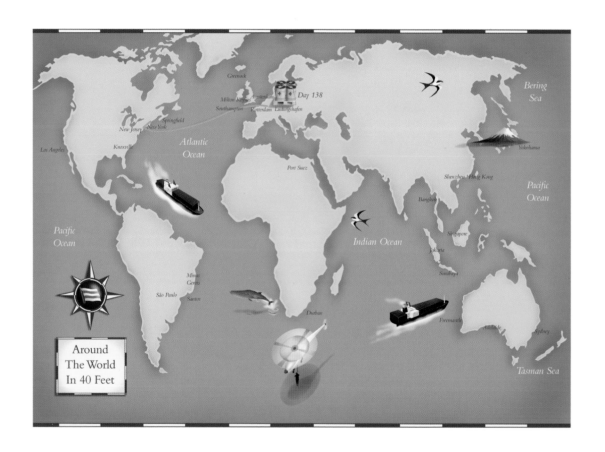

*Pharmaceuticals*
*Ludwigshafen–Rotterdam–New Jersey*

# Chapter 7

## DAY **142**, KILOMETER **87,435**
# ROTTERDAM, HOLLAND

Box 596079–1 is aboard the Cape Charles and is about to leave Rotterdam for New York. It's just after dusk and from up on the ship's bridge wing, the port is a myriad of sparkles – from the floodlights on the crane gantries, the headlights of the trucks continually crossing the wharves and the beams of the arc lights that, from a forest of high steel poles, send their strong sodium casts across the thousands of containers below.

Despite the constant clang of containers being lifted from stack to truck to crane and to ship, and the modern-day industrial sprawl that seems to go forever into the Dutch night, the port looks strangely beautiful on this cold yet clear evening. Captain David Rae, who is taking the ship to New York, looks out at the scene below him as the last few containers are loaded aboard the ship. It is scheduled to leave at 19.50 and will call at Le Havre and then Southampton before making the 5,000-plus-kilometer trip west, southwest across to the United States. There's an especially bad storm in the North Atlantic, which has meant delays for all ships making the crossing, and heavy snow is forecast along the East Coast of America.

Captain Rae, who is Scottish and has been sailing for more than 30 years, has been keeping a cautious eye on the reports of the rough weather ahead. "It's nothing this ship hasn't handled before," he says, tapping the metal deck with his foot, "but you can't ever be complacent. You never go looking for trouble."

The box has been in Europe for seven days. It arrived from Singapore aboard the NYK Lynx at Ceres Paragon, NYK's own terminal, situated just outside Amsterdam. All ships going to Amsterdam have to negotiate the series of canals and sea locks that have, for almost 100 years, protected this low-lying land from the North Sea's ever-present flooding menace. It's slow, meticulous work on the canals, so the Lynx took on two Dutch pilots who, as the 40-meter-wide ship painstakingly crept

through locks that were on occasion just 47 meters wide, stood on each bridge wing and vigilantly stared forward and down, carefully monitoring the portable GPS units that all Dutch pilots carry because of this tight, tricky work.

At Amsterdam the box was swiftly brought ashore. Ceres Paragon is a U-shaped terminal that sits off one of the sea canals, and its immense overhead loading cranes – which span the divide from both sides of the "U" – make it one of the fastest-working terminals in the world.

From Ceres Paragon the box was carried by road to a warehouse on the edge of the small town of Geldermaisen, 50 kilometers southeast of Amsterdam, where the 2,352 cartons of Australian Chardonnay were put straight onto pallets ready for immediate distribution to supermarkets across The Netherlands. The wine, shipped from an Adelaide winery less than three weeks ago, will be on Dutch shelves and in Dutch homes within the month.

From Geldermaisen, the empty box headed into the heart of industrial Germany, first to an NYK container yard outside Cologne then 160 kilometers south, then to an immense, self-contained, seven-square-kilometer chemical manufacturing complex in Ludwigshafen on the River Rhine.

There the box waited overnight before being loaded the next day with 18 tightly sealed drums of a highly specialized pharmaceutical compound, which will be shipped to the United States for more processing before ending up in hospitals across the country.

The complex, employing a staggering 39,000 people, has its own barge loading facility, where box NYKU 596079–1 was put aboard a river barge that took it directly into Rotterdam port, 600 kilometers back across the Dutch border. It spent three days aboard the barge gently heading west along the Rhine and another few hours in the storage stacks at Rotterdam, before being put on the Cape Charles at 16.04.

By 19.20, the last of the 1,420 containers loaded at Rotterdam is safely onboard and Captain Rae receives the message from his chief officer that the pilot has just come aboard and the ship is ready to get underway.

"Over the years, so much of this job has changed," he says, pointing out the thousands of gleaming containers that lie lined up along the Rotterdam quay. "But once you get out to sea again, it's almost the same as it always has been." And with that he gives the command to set sail before leaving to check, once again, the status of the storm in the North Atlantic.

The box arrived in New York aboard the Cape Charles, which came into the city's huge harbor under the Verrazano-Narrows Bridge. In front of the port's vast network of terminals, piers and wharves it was swung round by two tugs and berthed at Howland Hook Terminal on a crisp and clear Staten Island morning.

**ABOVE** – NYKU 596079–1 still on the deck of the Cape Charles just before it is brought ashore in New York. On this trip, the box will spend five days in the United States before it heads south to the far warmer climes of Brazil.

**OPPOSITE PAGE** – Truck driver Wascar Herrera grabs a hot coffee before he takes the container, full of pharmaceuticals, along the freezing highways of New Jersey. "There could be snow," he says. "And then one million people will be crossing from Manhattan trying to get out of the city."

## DAY **150**, KILOMETER **148,949**
# NEW YORK, USA

It's close to freezing in New York and Wascar Herrera pulls the fur-lined collar on his jacket high up around his neck, before jumping down from his truck to buy a hot coffee from a busy street-side wagon. He gulps down the coffee, clambers back up to the cab and turns the heaters on full. "Man, it's cold," he says as he blows into his hands.

On this crisp and clear New York morning, Wascar is taking the pharmaceuticals inside NYKU 596079–1 from a terminal on Staten Island the short way down the New Jersey Turnpike to a secure warehouse complex in Edison. Wascar estimates the journey should take about an hour but could take a lot more. "There could be snow," he says. "And then one million people will be crossing from Manhattan trying to get out of the city."

Wascar is typical of the hundreds of truckers who work the huge port area that stretches across New York and New Jersey. He works mainly short-haul deliveries within New Jersey and New York, taking full boxes from the terminals to warehouses and distribution centers and empty ones back to the yard at Newark, New Jersey. Sometimes he will spend his day shuttling empties between the yard and the port terminals.

Born in the Dominican Republic, Wascar has lived in New York for 13 years and speaks English with both a strong New York inflection and a clear Spanish accent. As he drives, one of the two mobile phones he carries – one for work and one for family – always seems to be ringing. Sometimes it's his depot controller asking about his progress or informing him of another job; sometimes it's his wife and he answers both using a wonderfully seamless weave of English and Spanish.

He says the work is okay but the very apparent step-up in security is a major hindrance to his daily life. "It's at the port gates, stop checks on the road… but what are you going to do?" Overall though, he says his life on the roads of New York and New Jersey is a good one.

Wascar works for a big New Jersey-based trucking outfit called Ironbound. The company, which does a lot of contract haulage work for NYK, is named after the tightly knit Newark dock area where it is based. Today, Ironbound is an area filled with block after block of container storage yards and although this is largely because of the area's proximity to both docks and highways, it is also in part because of history.

The area was once home to some of the best metal workshops in the New York area thanks to the high number of skilled southern European metalworkers who made the low-rent dockside area home after migrating to the States in the late 19th century.

When containerization first started developing in the middle of the 20th century, the knowledge of these European metalworkers was utilized to make the first prototypes, which makes Ironbound the birthplace of the shipping container.

Shipping container number NYKU 596079–1 arrived in New York, five kilometers from its ancestral home, early yesterday morning. The Cape Charles came into the city's huge harbor under the Verrazano-Narrows Bridge and in front of the port's extensive network of terminals, piers and wharves, was swung round by two tugs and berthed at Howland Hook at 07.28.

Almost 24 hours later, Wascar drove down to the terminal gate to queue in a long line of trucks waiting to enter the port to pick up their respective boxes. After waiting in line for three hours, which Wascar says is "not so bad – sometimes it can be six, sometimes more", he is on the road and heading south along the New Jersey Turnpike.

The snow he predicts does not come and he makes the trip down to Edison in just over an hour. The pharmaceuticals are plucked from the box within 30 minutes and before lunchtime he is ready to be back on the road, taking NYKU 596079–1 to the yard at Ironbound, where it will spend two days in storage before heading up to Massachusetts to pick up a load of glass resin destined for Brazil.

Before Wascar can roll his cab out of the yard and back onto the road, one of his phones – the family one – rings again. He answers it and after a brief exchange, conducted almost entirely in Spanish, he hangs up and then laughs out loud.

"My wife," he says. "She wants to know if I'm warm enough." He subconsciously checks his cab's heaters before swinging the enormous vehicle out onto the busy roads of New Jersey.

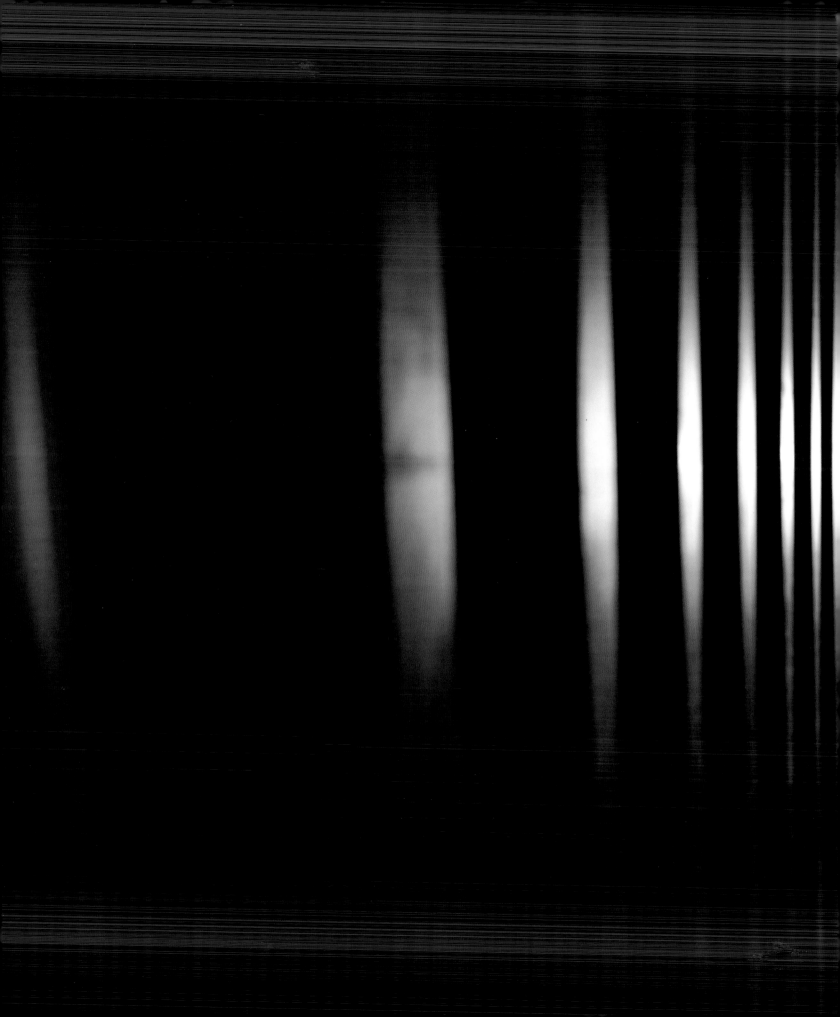

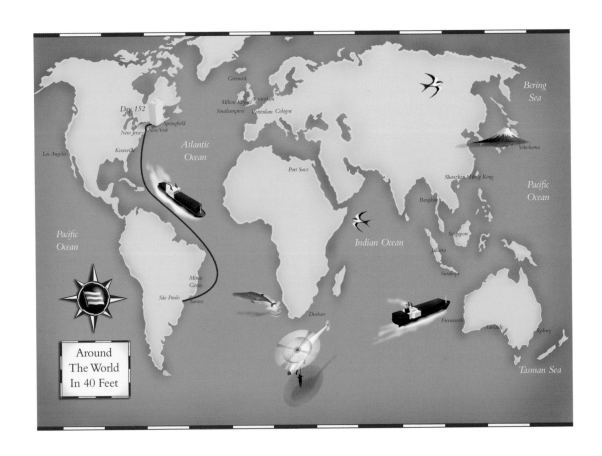

*Resin*
*Springfield–Santos–São José Dos Campos*

# Chapter 8

OPPOSITE PAGE – Box NYKU 596079–1 is quickly loaded with a resin compound at a leafy site in Connecticut and within a few hours is back on the road, heading for the Port of New York.

ABOVE – The Iwato takes on board its last containers in New York before it heads south for 8,000 kilometers. It will arrive in the Port of Santos, in southeast Brazil, after 15 days.

## DAY **169**, KILOMETER **101,914**
# SÃO JOSÉ DOS CAMPOS, BRAZIL

ox NYKU 596079–1 is in Brazil and it's humid; the air is still and the skies above are filled with ominously black rain clouds. Truck driver Paulo Antonio Viera looks at the heavens and curses: "The traffic will be terrible in São Paulo tonight."

It's approaching mid-afternoon and the container is sitting outside a spotless production plant in São José Dos Campos, about 130 kilometers to the northeast of São Paulo. The zone is one of the most modern and well-equipped industrial areas in Brazil and the production plant where NYKU 596079–1 now waits is part of a much bigger, highly secure and state-of-the-art compound that is home to dozens of similar such facilities. It's all very well ordered, immaculately clean and attractively landscaped with lawns, trees and small clumps of manicured shrubs; at first sight it could easily be mistaken for California, Japan or Northern Europe.

Box NYKU 596079–1 took 18 days to reach here. Its cargo of resin compound was packed into 18 tough, two-meter tall, multi-trip cage-like plastic bags, all especially palletized for the journey, and loaded into the container at a sprawling chemical manufacturing complex on the edge of the town of Springfield, just over the woody Massachusetts border from Connecticut. It's a beautiful yet industrial corner of the United States and the plant is a busy and efficient place that fills in excess of 100 containers a week. NYKU 596079–1's visit there was brief. It arrived at 07.30 and left again shortly after 09.00, traveling by road the 280-odd kilometers back to the port at New York where, one day later, it was loaded aboard the Brazil-bound NYK vessel, the Iwato.

The 4,850-kilometer passage from New York to the port of Santos took 15 days. After passing close to the northern tip of Bermuda and calling at Caucedo in the Dominican Republic, the ship came around Brazil's coastal shoulder, hugged the

shore and arrived at Santos, 80 kilometers outside the city of São Paulo. The box spent a day in the yard at the bustling port and was then carried, again by truck, across the astonishing stretch of steel and concrete that is home to about 30 million Paulistanos, from where it went up to São José Dos Campos.

The plant uses the resin to make a protective film for glass employed largely in car windscreens to stop them shattering, but it also has other uses, including making glass bullet proof. While the Massachusetts plant produces the raw resin ingredient, this more specialized facility processes it into the finished product, which leaves again in wide rolls of film sent to car manufacturing plants in squat, boxed pallets. The product may go anywhere across South America, or may even go back to the States or the Far East. It's part of a bigger "just-in-time" supply chain that stretches right across the planet; the raw ingredients for the film are ordered as they are needed, as is the finished product by the car manufacturers.

Box NYKU 596079–1 waits for a couple of hours outside the loading bay before being quickly unpacked. The hefty plastic bags are immediately taken from the interior of the box straight to the start of the production line, where they are hooked onto a gantry system, pulled above a tank and emptied, thus starting the complicated two-day process that will end with sheets of tough film.

Once emptied, the box heads back across a severely yet typically traffic-snarled São Paulo to Santos, where it waits, in an NYK storage yard near the port terminals, for one day. During this time it is washed and steam cleaned and then sent back on the road once again, traveling almost 750 kilometers to the north, up to the rolling hills of Minas Gerais.

The area is known in Brazil as one of the country's richest agricultural and mining regions, rich in beef, corn, soybeans, sugarcane and iron but it is especially famous for its coffee – exactly what box NYKU 596079–1 will pick up next.

While São José Dos Campos is a wonderful indicator of this country's modern, high-tech character, Minas Gerais is the classic, timeless version of Brazil. On the road, the container passes acres of lush green fields and brown, barefoot youths skilfully kicking soccer balls across bumpy dirt pitches; it passes carts pulled by donkeys, and, best of all, ancient roadside cantinas, where huge slabs of beef are cooked to tender perfection over smoky wood-burning stoves, then carved, slice after thick slice, at each diner's table. If it's a long way from São José Dos Campos, it's a million miles from Massachusetts.

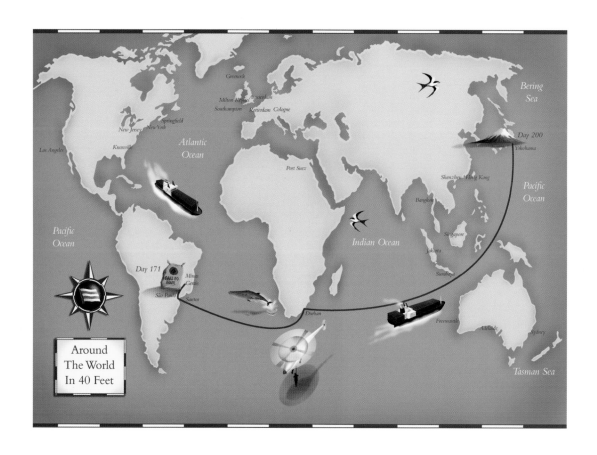

*Coffee Beans*
*Minas Gerais–Durban–Yokohama*

# Chapter 9

## DAY 171, KILOMETER 102,794
# MINAS GERAIS, BRAZIL

Walter Joaquim and Guilherme Mundin are standing side by side, assessing the quality of a small mound of unroasted coffee beans and both are clearly enjoying the process. Guilherme scoops his hands through the greenish beans and pulls an overflowing cluster up to his face before letting the beans fall back to the table. As they fall he buries his nose in the tumbling mass, breathes in, pauses for a moment and smiles. "Superb," he says.

The pair are in Minas Gerais, one of the finest coffee-growing regions on the planet. Walter, who is NYK Brazil's Senior Coffee Salesman – but is better known across the NYK world simply as "the coffee guy" – is here to check on a coffee shipment that will today leave this hilly and beautifully verdant area and head to the port at Santos, 720 kilometers away to the south. From there it will join the NYK Floresta and travel for more than 18,000 kilometers – across the South Atlantic, the Indian Ocean and the South and East China Seas – to Japan.

He is in the grading room of a coffee cooperative, where coffee is cleaned, assessed, packed and stored on behalf of a network of approximately 150 local independent farmers. Guilherme is the co-op's young, highly skilled and energetic chief grader. He has a raft of professional grading and judging qualifications from all over the world and the passion and enthusiasm he holds for all things coffee related are infectious. In the small, pristine room there are hundreds of samples of beans, all kept in little 300-gram circular tins that look similar to the cans in which movie film rolls are stored. Guilherme is eagerly showing Walter different samples from this year's harvest.

"Last year was superb in terms of volume and quality," he says. "So with this harvest we are expecting less. It is often the pattern – a low-yield year will follow a high-yield year – because the plants just cannot produce two bumper crops in a row. They

need time to recuperate," he says as he pulls another pile of beans up to his nose. "But this year's crop, although smaller, is still fantastic, right?" he asks with a fervent grin – and a few coffee beans – on his face.

Each year about 650,000 bags, each weighing 60 kilos, pass through the co-op. First they go through a series of sieves that clean and sort the beans according to size before they are graded according to quality, then bagged in traditional jute sacks and stacked, ready for export, in the co-op's cavernous, dark, cool warehouse. The coffee is assigned one of four grades and the best is always sent overseas, unroasted.

Opposite the grading room, across the co-op's wide, sun-kissed yard, sits NYKU 596079–1 with its doors open. A muscular yet jovial loading crew has arrived to fill the box tightly with 440 bags of top-grade, unroasted beans, but before any coffee can be put inside the interior walls of the box must be specially wrapped in tough brown craft paper. Although the box's interior was cleaned only two days ago at the NYK yard at Santos port, this procedure is a long-standing tradition in Brazil's coffee industry and every NYK box filled with coffee is given the exact same treatment: it prevents condensation affecting the precious cargo as it moves through different climates.

Four of the loading crew athletically leap into the container and cut the tall rolls of craft wrap into strips before swiftly stacking them from floor to ceiling. It takes them 10 minutes to dress the container, after which the box is backed up to the warehouse's tall wooden doors and a mobile conveyor belt is wheeled from the warehouse and into the back of the open container. The loading crew then jump to the task at hand and make impressively quick work of the weighty 60-kilo bags: within 40 minutes, all 440 bags are aboard.

All the coffee that is now inside NYKU 596079–1 has come from the same farm, 15 kilometers away from the warehouse in the small, picturesque village of Araguari. The farm is owned and run by Serafim Peres, an elderly soft-spoken farmer who runs what he describes as a medium-sized coffee-growing business. "Never more than 9,000 bags a year," he says.

Serafim also grows mangos, bananas and coconuts on his land, although those are a local sideline. Like Guilherme and so many others in the Minas Gerais region, it is coffee that is his main source of income and his enduring, life-long passion. He smiles warmly when told about the 440 bags inside NYKU 596079–1 that will end up in coffee houses across the greater Tokyo area. "I sincerely hope they enjoy it," he says.

ABOVE – At a coffee cooperative in Minas Gerais, in the heart of Brazil's beautiful rural interior, a warehouse crew fill NYKU 596079–1 with 440 bags of top-grade, unroasted coffee beans.

OPPOSITE PAGE – Before the coffee is loaded, the box's interior is dressed with craft wrap paper to prevent condensation affecting the beans as they move through different climates. Once this is done, the crew make impressively quick work of the weighty 60-kilo sacks, and within 40 minutes all 440 bags are loaded.

## DAY **183**, KILOMETER **110,029**
# DURBAN, SOUTH AFRICA

Box NYKU 596079–1 is off the coast of Africa and is delayed. The NYK Floresta has been sitting at the deep-sea anchorage 10 kilometers off Durban for two days. Durban is South Africa's busiest port, but despite recent terminal expansion there simply is not enough room for the number of ships that need to call there. Which means delays are common. Fourteen other ships sit at the anchorage with the Floresta, all waiting for the port's control tower to clear their entrance to the city's huge, natural and spectacular circular bay, protected from the Indian Ocean by a breakwater with a narrow, one-ship-at-a-time channel.

There are, however, far worse places in the world to be delayed. The weather out on this beautiful southeastern sweep of Africa is perfect. It's breezy and enjoyably warm with next to no humidity. Giant sea turtles go drifting by the ship, as does a family of whales that has been basking off the coast for the last three days.

While the crew have been using the break to carry out general maintenance duties – outside they have been painting sections of the deck, while in the engine room they have replaced one of the engine block covers – they have also had the chance to kick back a little. The fishing here is excellent and yesterday one of the crew caught a 12-kilo dogfish, which all 20 crew members enjoyed for dinner last night. They have also held a brief, impromptu concert while at anchor, led by the ever-resourceful ship's bosun, Arcadio Pragas, who has made a drum kit from old oil containers. As the sea gently rocked in the African offshore breeze, Arcadio and two of his shipmates belted out that modern-day seafarers' classic, "Sailing", much to the delight of everyone else on board.

"Yes, we're lucky. It's a good crew and a happy ship," says the Floresta's genial captain, Ukrainian Oleksander Kuzmenko, with a smile. "And that makes a huge difference."

He says part of the reason is the schedule. "We are busy in Brazil and busy in the Far East, then we have a long run in between. It's 10 days between Santos and Durban and then another 12 days up to Singapore. These days, it's actually quite rare to have that amount of time at sea and it's good – it gives everyone a chance to calm down a bit between ports."

Oleksander is on the bridge looking out across the cobalt blue ocean that surrounds him. He has been told he may receive the call to head in today or tomorrow and has just been talking via radio to Vernon Pillay, the NYK Operations Superintendent at Durban.

The Floresta is carrying a large electrical transformer that is to be off-loaded there. It came on board in Santos on a flatbed chassis and weighs just under 48 tonnes.

The terminal cranes can lift a maximum of 50 tonnes and Vernon wanted to make sure there will be no problems when the Floresta finally reaches port.

"It was fine coming on at Santos," says the captain after speaking to Vernon, "but if there are any problems the guys at the port say they will bring in a mobile crane that can lift up to 90 tonnes. We shouldn't need it but it's good to know it's there."

As Oleksander talks, a helicopter flashes by the ship and then hovers above a neighboring vessel. Durban port uses choppers to ferry pilots between shore and the deep-sea anchorage to help speed things up.

When a ship does receive clearance to go into port a helicopter can put a marine pilot on board within 10 minutes, whereas a launch takes an hour or more. And it also means the sailors can watch the performance of pilots being winched up and down from the decks and bridge wings of neighboring ships. "It's quite a show," says Oleksander, as he watches a winch through his binoculars.

The next morning the Floresta receives its call and at exactly the scheduled time the distinctive whir of rotor blades can be heard. Moments later, a helicopter hovers around the ship. A winch man points out of the chopper's open door to the crew below, showing where they will place the pilot, and within seconds the winching is complete.

Minutes later the ship is heading into harbor; 18 hours after that, it has off-loaded 842 containers – as well as one large transformer, without the use of the mobile crane – onto African soil and then the Floresta, with NYKU 596079–1 on board, is leaving Africa and heading for Asia.

**ABOVE –** As the NYK Floresta waits to enter the Port of Durban, the crew use the break to hold an impromptu concert. Bosun Arcadio Pragas (left) leads the band in a chorus of "Sailing" as the ship gently rocks in the offshore African breeze.

**OPPOSITE PAGE –** The men on the Floresta use the period spent at the deep sea Durban anchorage to carry out general deck and engine repairs – while also finding the time to enjoy a spot of fishing.

**ABOVE –** A marine pilot is winched down onto the deck of the NYK Floresta. Ten minutes after the winch, the helicopter is back on the pad at Durban and the marine pilot is sipping coffee on the Floresta's bridge, guiding the ship into harbor.

**OPPOSITE PAGE –** Port of Durban stevedores take a break before helping to unload 842 containers from the Floresta. For NYKU 596079–1, however, Durban is just a transit stop – the next time it touches dry land it will be in Yokohama.

## DAY **200**, KILOMETER **122,589**
# YOKOHAMA, JAPAN

It is cold in Yokohama; the sky is clear, bright and brilliant blue and box NYKU 596079–1 is at the storage yard at the NYK Yokohama Container Terminal. It's empty and has just been washed and now it sits with its doors tied slightly ajar as its interior dries in the strong ocean breeze.

The box has been in Japan for three days. It arrived at Yokohama aboard the NYK Floresta at dusk, as the huge glowing golden winter sun was slowly disappearing behind the distant, snow-covered Mount Fuji.

From the port, the box went on a short, five-kilometer journey around Yokohama Bay to a complex of low-rise modern warehouses, where it was backed into a loading bay before a team of helmeted workers gathered round, snipped its two plastic seals and gently swung open its high blue double doors. And, as the doors opened, the rich, aromatic smell of Brazilian coffee beans filled the crisp Japanese air.

Japan is tech-savvy, modern and pristine; yet while the setting is so utterly different from Brazil, some of the warehouse methodology is uncannily similar. The same sort of conveyor belt as the one deployed in Minas Gerais was pushed up to the edge of the container floor, and with the same universal set of whistles and shouts it was set into motion and the team began to unload the coffee. Each bag was weighed as it came out and its weight was scribbled in thick black marker on the sack's side before it was stacked and shunted into the adjoining warehouse.

Good, fresh coffee has long been an everyday passion in Japan and coffee shops are an ever-present feature of all downtown areas. The beans will once again be tested and graded here before being sent to roasting houses, then on to coffee shops across Tokyo.

Coffee traders the world over know the Japanese will pay a premium, but only for the very best beans. The process – from

container to coffee house – can take up to three months, but because Serafim Peres' coffee is likely to be given the highest grade here it will probably move along the chain much more quickly than that.

The Japanese team took about the same time to unload as the Brazilian team, and when finished they meticulously removed all the craft wrap that was stuck to the container walls 20,000 kilometers before. Box NYKU 596079–1 left the storage facility within an hour of arriving and headed back around the bay to the same terminal yard at which the Floresta docked. On arrival, it went straight into the cleaning and maintenance sheds.

All boxes that have carried coffee into Japan are washed when empty to remove their not unpleasant yet distinctive, pungent smell. First they are cold rinsed, then warm washed, and then their doors are tied open to allow them to dry before they are shifted back to the yard. There, before being returned to service, they are checked inside and out for damage.

Box NYKU 596079–1 is inspected and has, on one of its recent journeys, received a small dent on one of the corners of its underbelly. It may have happened when it was loaded onto the Floresta in Brazil; it could have been when it was placed onto Wascar's truck at Staten Island; when it was put on the barge on the Rhine in Germany; or when it was loaded aboard the Lynx in the driving rain in Singapore… or it may even have been before that.

Either way, Toshio Kosugi, a maintenance welder at the yard, has seen the dent, and although the damage is minor he has decided it is significant enough to repair. So he has the box taken into the huge repair sheds, pulls it into the air using a powerful winch, places it on a set of hefty metal trestles and goes to work, first cutting into the indentation with a set of large grinders, then re-welding the steel until smooth.

The NYK maintenance team at Yokohama Container Terminal, which includes painters, carpenters and welders, deals on a daily basis with containers that have, on their global marathons, received bounces, bangs, knocks, scrapes, spills and occasionally even burns. The work Toshio has to do on NYKU 596079–1 is straightforward and quick for him. The box is patched and repainted and ready to leave the shed within two hours.

Once finished, Toshio steps back from the box to admire his work. "It's a sound box again," he says, tapping the container's side. "Good for another few hundred thousand kilometers."

**LEFT –** NYKU 596079–1 arrives in Japan at the NYK Yokohama Container Terminal, before making a three-kilometer trip round Yokohama Bay to a complex of low-rise modern warehouses. There the box's doors are opened, and the rich, aromatic smell of Brazilian coffee beans fills the sharp Japanese air.

**OPPOSITE PAGE –** Despite being a world away, a lot of the warehouse methodology used in Japan is similar to that seen in Brazil: the same sort of conveyor belt as the one deployed in Minas Gerais is pushed up to the edge of the container floor and with the same set of whistles and shouts, the conveyor belt is set in motion and the team starts to unload the coffee.

**ABOVE –** Once the bags are unloaded, box NYKU 596079–1, like all containers that have carried coffee, is cleaned to remove the distinctive aroma from its interior. First it is cold rinsed, then warm washed, then its doors are tied open to allow it to dry in the breeze.

**OPPOSITE PAGE –** The box has picked up a small dent on its underbelly and before it is returned to service, maintenance welder Toshio Kosugi undertakes the repairs. Within hours the box is repainted and is ready for another journey… to somewhere in the world.

**Around the World in 40 Feet**

*First published in Hong Kong in 2007 by WordAsia Limited, Hong Kong, on behalf of NYK Group, Tokyo*

*Text and concept: Richard Cook*
*Photography: Marcus Oleniuk*
*Editing: Stephen McCarty and Louisa Wah Hansen*
*Consultant editors: Sam Chambers and Matthew Flynn*
*Design: Yuen Ling Chung and Tilly Johnson*
*Map illustrations: Harry Harrison*

*NYK Project Editor: Terry Takasaki*
*NYK Regional Editors – Hong Kong: Jonathan Chiu*
*Johannesburg: Jerry Hookins*
*London: Ian Aitchison and Katherine Dodd*
*New York: Doug Cole*
*São Paulo: Masaki Osawa and Arne Bengtsson*
*Singapore: Lawrence Liaw*
*Sydney: Lenny Lee*

*ISBN-978-988-97392-3-2*
*www.nyk.com*
*www.wordasia.com*